Praise for

THE HUMANITY OF MUHAMMAD

"It is certain that the most dangerous shared enemy of ours is ignorance. Hence the Holy Qur'an emphasizes on the importance of knowledge. And that includes the imminent importance of "*ta'aruf*" (knowing one another).

"I am deeply thankful and highly appreciative of the inclusive thoughts Dr. Craig has demonstrated and continues to promote. His honesty in his scholarly pursuit, I assume, is widely challenged by his own community of faith.

"In this book once again he demonstrates his openness, inclusiveness and his sincere and honest view about our Prophet Muhammad, peace be upon him. That Prophet Muhammad (pbuh) is truly a role model for our pursuit of peace, justice and happiness for our common humanity."

—Imam Shamsi Ali
Spiritual Leader of Jamaica Muslim Center
President of Nusantara Foundation

"I was impressed that Craig begins his book by talking about the persecution of Christians in Muslim-majority countries as a backdrop to what Muhammad's message really is, opening up the difficult conversation that he proposes. It is a few steps from here to the Christian delegation that Muhammad welcomed to his mosque in Medina and the early Muslim delegation which took refuge with the Christian king of Abyssinia. This book is a reminder that Muhammad's vision was of diverse religious communities living side by side in peace and harmony."

—Julian Bond
Former Director of the Christian Muslim Forum, United Kingdom

"In today's world, we need bridge builders and peacemakers. Dr. Considine's book is timely and needed in order to create a better understanding between those who don't know much about Islam and its Prophet ﷺ and their Muslim neighbors. The book tackles important topics that are well-chosen and necessary if we are to re-place ignorance with knowledge and hatred with love. I found the information accurate and based on our best available references.

"I highly recommend this book to anyone who wants to seriously learn about Prophet Muhammad ﷺ and who wants to draw from the gifts of wisdom and enlightenment that the Prophet ﷺ brought into humanity."

— **Safi Kaskas**

Co-author of *The Qur'an, A Contemporary Understanding, with References to the Bible*

"Since the tragic attacks of September 11, 2001, Americans have been fed a steady diet of Islamophobia. Through media, social media, and even the pulpits of American churches, Muslims have been transformed into the 'other' and rendered incompatible with the 'Judeo-Christian' worldview and the secular values of Western civilization. My work with the Muslims of the World platform has been an effort to counteract this 'clash of civilizations' treatment of Muslims. But critical scholarship of this issue, particularly by Christian and Jewish scholars, is also vital to turn back the tide of Islamophobia. Muslims are in desperate need of Christian allies who are free of the racist and xenophobic effects of virulent Islamophobia and who have examined Islam and the life of Prophet Muhammad, peace be upon him, with historical honesty and academic rigor. Professor Craig Considine's *The Humanity of Muhammad: A Christian View* is the fruit of such scholarship. The result of Professor Considine's work is a reclaiming of the view that there is in fact a Judeo-Christian-Muslim theologic tradition and that the Prophet Muhammad (pbuh) was an egalitarian and an advocate of religious pluralism. Additionally, the Prophet Muhammad (pbuh) was deeply committed to the creation of just societies devoid of racism. Professor Considine does a wonderful job of analyzing the actual historical events of the life of the Prophet Muhammad (pbuh) through the lens of sociology and making the case for his embrace of his Christian neighbors and egalitarian worldview. It is a remarkable academic effort to help bring an end to the dangerous worldview of those who view Islam as a threat to the Judeo-Christian tradition and the values of Western Civilization. *The Humanity of Muhammad: A Christian View* is a well-researched, well-written invitation to instead begin an authentic Dialogue of Civilizations.

—Sajjad Shah
Founder of Muslims of the World
Author of *Muslims of the World*

"Craig Considine's *The Humanity of Muhammad: A Christian View* provides a welcome antidote to the hostility towards Islam and Muslims that permeates popular sentiment. His is a very sympathetic account of the compatibility between Islam and the civic values of pluralism, equality, education and social justice. By opening our hearts and minds to Muslims, Christians might have something to learn, and much that we can do together to make for a better world."

—Rev. Dr. Patrick McInerney
Director of the Columban Centre for
Christian-Muslim Relations in Australia

THE HUMANITY OF MUHAMMAD

A Christian View

Craig Considine

Blue Dome Press

New Jersey

Published by Blue Dome Press
335 Clifton Ave.
Clifton, NJ, 07011, USA
www.bluedomepress.com

Second edition
Hardcover: 978-1-68206-529-7
Ebook: 978-1-68206-530-3

Library of Congress Cataloging-in-Publication Data

Names: Considine, Craig, author.
Title: The humanity of Muhammad : a Christian view / Craig Considine.
Description: Clifton : Blue Dome Press, 2020. | Includes bibliographical
    references and index.
Identifiers: LCCN 2020011967 (print) | LCCN 2020011968 (ebook) | ISBN
    9781682065297 (hardcover) | ISBN 9781682065303 (ebook)
Subjects: LCSH: Muḥammad, Prophet, -632. | Islam--Relations--Christianity.
    | Christianity and other religions--Islam.
Classification: LCC BP75 .C655 2020 (print) | LCC BP75 (ebook) | DDC
    297.6/3--dc23
LC record available at https://lccn.loc.gov/2020011967
LC ebook record available at https://lccn.loc.gov/2020011968

CONTENTS

"There is a hidden sea of goodness that is growing and leads us to hope in dialogue, reciprocal knowledge and the possibility of building, together with the followers of other religions and all men and women of goodwill, a world of fraternity and peace."
– Pope Francis

FOREWORD

In the "Western world" today, much remains unknown about the world's second largest populated religion – Islam. In absence of knowledge, some think of Islam as a political ideology bent upon world domination, and some consider it an oppressive and/or violent doctrine contrary to the freedoms and values we cherish in the 21st century. Surely, everyone is entitled to their own judgment, but some are making judgments based on anything but facts and personal experience. Without meeting a Muslim or studying the faith and history of Islam from reputable peer-reviewed sources, they rely on news headlines, biased blogs, and online memes to formulate their opinions.

Amidst this climate of complacency, there are still rare gems who refuse to accept the warped narrative at face value. Instead, they pursue scholarship and independent research to truly understand matters at a more sophisticated level. Dr. Craig Considine is one such gem and an incredibly valuable resource for us all. As a devout Catholic, he has retained his Christian identity while studying the theology of Islam and recognizing it for what it is – a faith that seeks to formulate and foster within each believer a loving relationship with God and His creation. Once a skeptic about Islam, Dr. Considine studied it and the Holy Qur'an (its scripture) only to discover that his preconceived notions were inaccurate. From there, he had the integrity not only to embark on a genuine pursuit of truth regarding Islam and its teachings but also to share his research with the world with the purpose of breaking down self-imposed barriers of misunderstanding. I have had the pleasure to work with Dr. Considine and see the remarkable positive influence he has had on his students and readers.

Why is this important? Why should you care? The answer is all around us. The world is steeped in war, violence, conflict, chaos and disorder. The power-hungry exert their influence to divide and conquer. They leverage any label – nationality, ethnicity, economic class, religion, gender, political identity – to convince people they are better than "others," who must be confronted (or controlled) to protect one's own identity. Innumerable political, religious, social and media leaders have not simply highlighted the heinous acts of violence committed by those calling themselves Muslims; they have relied on the general ignorance of Islam to convince masses that Islam is the problem and does not align with modern ideals of peace.

When 62% of Americans don't know a Muslim and only have such leaders who spread false fears about Islam, of course they are bound to accept that rhetoric as the truth. This fear has provided the fertile soil for hatred to grow. For this reason, Dr. Considine's work is the much-needed antidote of our time. His careful examination of the true history of Islam and its Prophet Muhammad enriches his audience with greater knowledge and an appreciation for pluralism and building bridges of understanding between all people.

I hope you enjoy this journey through his work, and join the movement against racism and for pluralism.

Harris Zafar
Author of *Demystifying Islam: Tackling the Tough Questions*

Preface

I wrote this book to build stronger bridges of understanding and peace between Christians and Muslims, to uplift our common humanity, and to defend the honor of Prophet Muhammad, who has been depicted by many Christians throughout history as the anti-thesis of Jesus.

Over the last decade I have come to learn that the widespread mistrust between Christians and Muslims is unnecessary as well as antithetical to our shared Abrahamic traditions. *The Humanity of Muhammad: A Christian View* shows that Christians and Muslims have a long history of building authentic relationships based on common ideals and principles, and that a key reason for the formation of these relationships is the life and legacy of Muhammad himself.

I hope that the Muslims who read this book feel encouraged about the prospect of better relations between Christians and Muslims in the future, both in the "Western world" and the "Muslim world." My wish is that *The Humanity of Muhammad* will further open the hearts and minds of Muslims so that they may be able to view Christians in a more humane light. Christians, after all, are referred to as among the "People of the Book" in the Holy Qur'an, which also praises the humility of Christians: "And you will most certainly find that the nearest of them in affection to the believers (the Muslims) are those who say: 'We are Christians.' This is because there are among them (the Christians) hermits (who devote themselves to worshipping God, especially at night) and monks (who struggle with their carnal selves, ever fearful of God's punishment), and because they are not arrogant" (Qur'an 5:82).

The bigger challenge is that the following pages effectively reach the hearts and minds of Christians who hold sensational views of the Islamic tradition, Muslims themselves, and the Prophet Muhammad. I am confident that the words to come will galvanize Christians to embrace and even to love Muslims, for love is what Jesus commanded of his followers.

My Christian faith pushes me to encounter the Islamic tradition and Muslims themselves with respect, compassion, and peace. Christians completely miss the point of Jesus's teachings if they do not embody and live these principles in their everyday lives.

Acknowledgments

This book would not have been possible without the loving friendships that I have formed over the years with Muslims around the world. They have embraced me with open arms. They have welcomed me into their mosques, homes, schools, businesses, organizations, and neighborhoods. They have taken care of me and, perhaps more importantly, they have inspired me to be a better Christian. Indeed, Muslims have made me a better human being. There is no doubt in my mind about that.

INTRODUCTION

I remember September 11th, 2001 (henceforth 9/11) like it was yesterday. I was a sixteen-year-old student at Needham High School in Massachusetts. Mr. Walker, a history teacher, interrupted the American Legal System class that I was sitting in and whispered briefly to Ms. Nielson, my teacher, who said to our class: "One of the World Trade Center towers has been hit by a plane." Ms. Nielson did not seem too concerned about the event.

"Maybe there were mechanical problems on the plane," one student uttered to me. I remember hearing another student say – "Maybe the weather was just bad."

I, myself, had no immediate insight. I hardly even knew what the World Trade Center towers looked like or where they were even located.

As you can imagine, Mr. Walker ended up coming back into our classroom when the second plane hit the World Trade Center, except this time he seemed panicked and concerned. "It looks like we are under attack," he said to Ms. Nielson, whose demeanor was much different this time around. Mr. Walker then invited the class to join his class next door.

About fifty students crammed into a single classroom. We collectively watched the events of 9/11 unfold. It was a surreal moment. The thunderous noise of military jets could be heard flying over our school building. I had to quickly leave the room to call my mom, Debbie, to see if my dad, Christopher, was okay. He was set to fly from Boston to New York that morning. I had no idea about the location of his final destination. Thankfully, he was fine. His flight was cancelled once the Towers were struck.

I distinctly remember what happened when we left the classroom and entered the hallways. I heard my peers, a few of whom were my friends, saying things like "f**k the towelheads" and "screw those sand n****rs." Chants of "USA! USA" were louder and more enthusiastic than usual.

I knew practically nothing about the Islamic tradition or the Prophet on 9/11. Never once had I ever even met a Muslim.

Needham, the town that I grew up in, is a suburb of Boston with a population of approximately 30,000 people and composed primarily of white Catholics and Protestants. Churches dot the town including those of the Baptist, Catholic, Christian Science, Episcopalian, Lutheran, Presbyterian, and Unitarian traditions. Needham also has a sizeable Jewish population with two temples – Beth Shalom and Aliyah. The closest mosque to Needham is located about nine miles away in Roxbury, a predominantly African American neighborhood of Boston.

I graduated from Needham High School in 2003, the year that the United States and its allies decided to invade Iraq to topple the regime of Saddam Hussein. Around this time in my life, I started to closely follow domestic politics and international relations. The Iraq War was a constant fixture in media coverage, most of which was slanted to depict the Americans as the "good guys" and the Iraqis as "bad guys." Most Americans were fed a stream of news on how the Iraqi state had "weapons of mass destruction," and that they were ready to use these weapons against U.S. forces in the Middle East.

When it came time for me to pick an academic subject, I decided to study the "Muslim world" in order to figure out why something like 9/11 happened. I enrolled in Arabic language courses and several introductory courses about the Islamic faith. The main question on my mind, and the minds of many Americans at the time, was "Why do they hate us?" My goal in studying these subjects was to graduate from college with a degree so that I can enter the U.S. intelligence community, perhaps as an employee for the Central Intelligence Agency (CIA) or the Federal Bureau of Investigation (FBI).

The first time I learned about the Islamic faith from a source outside of the media was in 2006, when I enrolled in the course "The World of Islam" at American University in Washington, D.C. I was 19-years-old at the time. The professor of the course, Akbar Ahmed, opened the first day of class with a simple, but profound saying: "The ink of the scholar is more sacred than the blood of the martyr." This *hadith*[1] of Prophet Muhammad shook me to my core. It challenged my belief that there was something inherently violent about the Islamic faith and Muslims at large. It pushed me to think about the "Muslim world" beyond the lens of 9/11. And perhaps most importantly, this *hadith* opened my mind to the power of knowledge and the idea that our hearts and minds can be easily shaped by public discourse, news media, and worse, propaganda coming from governments.

Reflecting back on these experiences makes me wonder what could have happened to me if I entered a different class, with a different teacher. What if "The World of Islam" course was taught by a person who viewed the 9/11 events as a true reflection of the Islamic faith and Muhammad's teachings?

In reflecting back on these days of my life, I realize how easy it is for human beings to retreat into their comfort zones and state of ignorance. Many people are unable to transcend the walls of their own egos, and the assumptions of their own immediate social circles. How can we collectively rise from this lower state of being?

By gaining knowledge and uplifting our common humanity.

Seeking *'ilm*

I also learned in "The World of Islam" that the Qur'anic revelation started with the verse "Read in and with the Name of your Lord" (96:1), which was revealed by Angel Gabriel to Muhammad, an unlettered man, like most people in the society of the time. The term "read," or *iqra* in Arabic, is a poignant reminder that the very foundation of the Islamic faith is rooted in knowledge and scholarship. In fact, the Holy Qur'an has approximately 300 references to "using your mind." *'Ilm*, the word for knowledge, is featured more than any other word in the Islamic holy text apart from *Allah*, or God.[2] Even to this day Muhammad's words and Qur'anic verses serve as a reminder that the Islamic faith has a long history of harboring the most profound respect for the work of scholars and those seeking a path of enlightenment through education.[3]

The emphasis that Muhammad placed on seeking knowledge and learning in general inspired me to carry out research on his legacy in the hope of growing both as a person of faith and scholar. In the early years of my studies I explored the idea that Jews, Christians, and Muslims were like a "super tribe" rooted in Abraham. I quickly learned as an undergraduate student that these three sects of monotheism share many similarities, including belief in the oneness of God, the divine revelation of the prophets, the angels, the shared sacred history of God's encounter with humanity, and Judgment Day (Considine 2019: 1).

The early years of my studies at American University was a period of time when the term "Judeo-Christian" entered into the public discourse. Following 9/11, many critics claimed that "Islamic civilization" and "Islamic values" were fundamentally at odds with "Western civilization" and "Western values," as well as Judaism and Christianity at large. As a young scholar studying the similarities among the monotheistic faiths, I often became a bit puzzled as to why the Islamic faith was not considered part of the "Judeo-Christian" tradition. Why could there not be a Judeo-Christian-Islamic worldview or system of thought? Why are Muslims excluded from the fold of this tradition even as Muhammad himself deliberately stated, as informed by God, that the Islamic faith is not a "new faith," but a continuation of the Holy Bible, which came before the Holy Qur'an?[4]

Along with the Abrahamic tradition the term "clash of civilizations" was a topic of interest for me in my early years of studying Christian-Muslim relations. The clash of civilizations was popularized by Harvard University scholar Samuel Huntington following the demise of the Soviet Union during the 1990s. Huntington claimed that the main future conflict in the world would not be one between capitalists and communists, but rather civilizations and the cultures positioned within them.

"Islamic civilization," for Huntington, was of particular concern. To drive home his point on fearing Islam, Huntington's book *The Clash of Civilizations and the Remaking of World Order* (2011) had two flags juxtaposed on the cover. One flag represented the flag of the United States of America. The other flag showed a white crescent and star against a green background, an image often associated with the "Muslim world."

The clash of civilizations theory continued to gain prominence as I progressed in my studies. During the presidency of Barack Obama a fear of the *sharia*, or Islamic law, gained steam around the United States of America. State and local governments initiated many bills that would effectively ban elements of the *sharia*, and thus would criminalize certain practices of the Islamic faith (Considine 2018: 97-102). Years later, during the 2016 presidential election campaign, the clash of civilizations theory again became prominent in light of the rise of Da'esh, the "Muslim Ban," and anti-Muslim rhetoric. Several key political figures in the country referred to fear of Muslims and the Islamic faith as "rational."[5] Other prominent figures described the Islamic faith as one that had fascist tendencies, like the Nazi regime of Adolf Hitler before and during World War II.

In opposition to the clash of civilizations is the dialogue of civilizations. According to Turan Kayaoglu, a scholar on Christian-Muslim relations, the dialogue of civilizations is a "post-Cold War approach to international politics to acknowledge the importance of religious and cultural diversity in international society." He described it further as a theory that "claims to promote the role of culture and religion in conflict prevention and global peace" (Kayaoglu 2012: 129). The dialogue of civilizations stresses symbiotic interactions and the interpenetration of cultures and civilizations by deliberately creating spaces in which scholars, philosophers, and artists from different backgrounds interact with each other. At the heart of the paradigm is a respect for minority communities and those positioned outside of circles of power.

The concept of the dialogue of civilizations was touched upon by Mohammad Khatami, the former president of Iran, during a session at the United Nations in the aftermath of 9/11. Khatami encouraged human beings to realize the dialogue of civilizations by engaging in "an interaction and interpretation of cultures and civilizations with each other" and deliberately entering into dialogue "among representative members of various civilizations such as scholars, artists, and philosophers from disparate civilizational domains" (Khatami 2001: 26).

Pope Francis has recently taken the torch of the dialogue of civilizations and moved it forward in terms of building strong bridges among members of the Abrahamic tradition. Reflecting on his inter-actions with Muslims in Abu Dhabi, Francis said that his trip opened a new page in relations between Christians and Muslims, a page that stressed dialogue, brotherhood, and human fraternity, as captured in a statement he made in Rome:

> In an age like ours, in which there is a strong temptation to see a clash between Christian and Islamic civilizations taking place, and also to consider religions as sources of conflict, we wanted to give another clear and decisive sign that, on the contrary, it is possible to meet, re-spect, and dialogue with each other, and that, despite the diversity of cultures and traditions, the Christian and Islamic worlds appreciate and protect common values: life, the family, religious belief, honor for the elderly, the education of young people and much more (See Arocho Esteves 2019b).

So, which worldview will rise in the future – the clash of civi-lizations or the dialogue of civilizations? It is my intention to argue in this book that the dialogue of civilizations has strong roots in the history of Christian and Muslim relations, and that a primary rea-son for this reality is the vision that Prophet Muhammad laid out in Mecca and Medina in the 7th century.

Why this Christian is an "Islamic apologist"

Secret Muslim. Leftist. Liberal. Propagandist. People hurl these terms at me on what feels like an hourly basis via my social media pages. These terms are overused and misused so much that they no longer seem to have any meaning to me. To be clear, I do not self-identify with any of these identity labels. Placing me – or indeed anyone – into these categories is counterproductive. I am none of these things.

But there is another term thrown at me that I actually relate to as a scholar, Christian, and human being. That term is "Islamic apologist."

Before I explain why I am an Islamic apologist, let us first take a deeper look into the word "apology." The term comes from the Greek word *apologia*, which in short means "to give a defense." A classic case of apologetics is the *Apology of Socrates* by Plato, who presents the self-defense speech that Socrates[6] made at his trial for allegedly corrupting the youth of Athens. In the context of this book, apologetics is the science of defending the Islamic faith as well as the life and legacy of Muhammad.

It is no secret that this world of ours is filled with Islamophobes who bash the Holy Qur'an and defame Prophet Muhammad. These Islamophobes tend to treat the Islamic faith as a monolith, call it evil, and defend the persecution and even killing of Muslims worldwide. The mission of an Islamic apologist is to combat Islamophobia and promote better understanding of – and love for – the Holy Qur'an and the life of Prophet Muhammad. We might, then, define Islamic apologetics as follows:

> The task of articulating and sharing a wide spectrum of knowledge to shed light on the truth of the Islamic faith, to counteract falsehood, and to strengthen our common humanity.

For me, serving as an "Islamic apologist" is a process that involves presenting the essential truths about the Islamic faith to those who may have preconceived judgments about the Holy Qur'an, *Hadith*, Prophet Muhammad, and Muslims in general.

There are two primary methods of Islamic apologetics. The first involves sharing passages of the Holy Qur'an which give clear evidence that the Islamic faith is fundamentally rooted in mercy, compassion, and freedom, as seen in the following Qur'anic verses:

> "O mankind! Surely We have created you from a single (pair of) male and female, and made you into tribes and families so that you may know one another (and so build mutuality and co-operative relationships, not so that you may take pride in your differences of race or social rank, or breed enmities). Surely the noblest, most honorable of you in God's sight is the one best in piety, righteousness, the reverence for God. Surely God is All-Knowing, All-Aware" (49:13).

> "There is no compulsion in religion. The right way stands there clearly distinguished from the false." (2:256).

The second involves shining a light on the peaceful example of Muhammad to counteract anti-Islam and anti-Muslim rhetoric.

Here are several passages from the *Hadith* that shed light on Muhammad's teachings on peace:

> "O People! Spread peace, feed the hungry, and pray at night when people are sleeping and you will enter Paradise in peace" (Sunan Ibn Majah).
>
> "Verily, the best of the people to God are those who begin the greeting of peace" (Sunan Abu Dawud).
>
> "The most hated person in the sight of God is the most quarrelsome person" (Sahih Bukhari).
>
> "You will not enter Paradise until you believe and you will not believe until you love each other. Shall I show you something that, if you did, you would love each other? Spread peace among yourselves" (Sahih Bukhari).

The pluralist vision of Muhammad

If an Islamic apologist is someone who appreciates the way that Muhammad treated Christians, then you can consider me an apologist. Consider the visit of the Christians of Najran to Muhammad's mosque in Medina in 631, as I described in a *Middle East Eye* article:

> Picture this. A Muslim leader reaches out to a group of Christians and invites them to his country. The Christians happily accept the invitation, while the Muslim leader prepares his people for their arrival. This is the first time the two communities have met in an official delegation. Matters of state, politics and religion are the topics of discussion. The two groups see eye-to-eye on most issues, but also agree to disagree on theological issues. If one phrase can best describe their meeting, it is "mutual respect."
>
> At the end of their talks, the Christians tell the Muslims, "It is time for us to pray." The problem for the Christians is that there is no church nearby to worship. Instead of letting the Christians pray on the dirty street, the Muslim leader tells the Christians, "You are followers of the one true God, so please come pray inside my mosque. We are all brothers in humanity." The Christians agree to use the "Islamic space" as their own. A bridge between these religious communities is made in the name of peace and goodwill.

This story is not some fairytale. It is a historical fact (I did, however, make-up quotes based on how the interaction might have played out). The Muslim leader of the story is Prophet Muhammad and the Christians are from Najran, or modern-day Yemen. The event happened in Medina in 631. This moment in time represents one of the first examples of Muslim-Christian dialogue, but more importantly, one of the first acts of religious pluralism in Islamic history (Considine 2016b).

Unfortunately, Islamophobes completely neglect this story. Instead, they tend to take Qur'anic passages out of context to claim that Muhammad persecuted the Christians in his midst. And, ironically, groups like Da'esh, al-Qaeda, and their sympathizers carry out the same method as Islamophobes – they literally interpret Qur'anic verses without any sense of historical or contemporary context.

Claiming that the Prophet would support the demolition of churches, as Islamophobes claim, has no credibility in light of his Covenants with Christians. In these treaties, Muhammad stated that Christians living within the realm of the Islamic state are granted freedom of religion and freedom of conscience. Going beyond religious tolerance, the Prophet in fact advocated for religious pluralism. He commanded Muslims to engage in dialogue with Christians, and demanded they interact with them in a respectful and egalitarian way.

As a Christian, I do not simply respect these kinds of teachings. I love them.

An honest analysis of the Holy Qur'an and *Hadith* – as well as the Prophet's interactions with Christian communities around him – remind us that Christians are indeed "People of the Book." Islamic scripture proclaims that Christians have received revelation from God's prophets and that they share commonalities with Muslims. The Holy Qur'an states:

> Those who believe (i.e. professing to be Muslims), or those who declare Judaism, or the Christians or the Sabaeans (or those of some other faith) whoever truly believes in God and the Last Day and does good, righteous deeds, surely their reward is with their Lord, and they will have no fear, nor will they grieve (Qur'an 2:62).

Surely, be they of those who declare faith (the Community of Muhammad), or be they of those who are the Jews or the Sabaeans or the Christians (or of another faith) whoever truly and sincerely believes in God and the Last Day and does good, righteous deeds they will have no fear, nor will they grieve (Qur'an 5:69).

... And You will most certainly find that the nearest of them in affection to the believers (the Muslims) are those who say: 'We are Christians.' This is because there are among them (the Christians) hermits (who devote themselves to worshipping God, especially at night) and monks (who struggle with their carnal selves, ever fearful of God's punishment), and because they are not arrogant" (Qur'an 5:82).

Millions upon millions of Muslims around the world love these verses. They defend these messages because Muhammad commanded them too. How can a Christian – or any person of faith, for that matter – not defend that?

No matter what religion you may adhere to, we are all commanded by the prophets who came before us to spread goodwill to our neighbors, and even to strangers and enemies. That is the essence of being Muslim, that is the essence of being Christian, and that is most definitely the essence of being human. To that I say: "Peace."

Structure of the book

This book is academic in nature, but it is also written in an accessible manner for the general public. People that may be interested in this piece of scholarship include, but is by no means limited to: religious leaders, community organizers, politicians, activists, academics, teachers, and those involved in interreligious dialogue.

Chapter 1 explores Muhammad's preference for religious pluralism by means of his relations with the Christians of Najran, the Covenant with the Christian monks of Mount Sinai, and the first *hijrah* to the Christian kingdom of Abyssinia.

Chapter 2 focuses on the notion of civic nation state building, which I argue is the Prophet's preferred system of nation building for the *ummah* as a way of fostering solidarity and social cohesion.

Further, I focus in this chapter on the similarities between the vision of Muhammad and the U.S. Founding Fathers in the hope of synthesizing "Islamic values" and "American values."

Chapter 3 addresses the rise of racism and racial inequalities around the world as perpetuated by politicians and other influential world leaders. Muhammad's example of anti-racism is distinguished from merely non-racism through his relationship with Bilal ibn Rabah, one of the Prophet's most trusted companions. Moreover, Muhammad's Farewell Sermon is used to explore his vision of racial equality in the *ummah*. The Prophet's example and teachings on racial equality are also examined in a historical manner to understand how Muslim nations have approached race and diversity.

Chapter 4 stresses the importance that Muhammad placed on seeking knowledge and how the inventions of Muslims played a prominent role in the development of world civilization. This chapter pinpoints the historical contributions that Muslim communities and leaders have made towards the development of humanity in the realms of higher learning, philosophy, and science. Several case studies are deployed to frame the analysis including the confluence of cultures in Sicily and the comparable philosophies of Rumi and Ralph Waldo Emerson.

Chapter 5 draws the reader's attention to Muhammad's relationship with women and the approach that he took in terms of granting women full and equal rights within the *ummah*. The chapter also examines the present-day matter of *hijab* and a women's right to observe this religious practice.

Chapter 6 aims to uplift spirits by learning about the Golden Rule and Muhammad's kindness, mercy, and humility. Jesus and Muhammad's teachings on the Golden Rule are reviewed in order to connect the lives of prophets who are revered by Christians and Muslims alike.

This book wraps up with a conclusion that provides my personal views on the prophethood of Muhammad and some recommendations on how human beings can move forward in a way that strengthens our common humanity.

CHAPTER ONE

RELIGIOUS PLURALISM

I t is no secret that Christians are persecuted in Muslim-majority countries. In fact, the situation for Christians in certain parts
of the world is dire. Experts believe that Christians are fast approaching the point of extinction from the Middle East, the very
region that housed the first Christian communities.

Open Doors,[7] for example, consistently ranks countries in the
Middle East among the worst for Christians to live in around the
world. In Saudi Arabia, Open Doors reports that Christians are
forced to practice and gather in a shroud of secrecy, if they gather at
all. The United States Commission on International Religious Freedom (USCIRF) noted in a 2019 report that Saudi Arabia remained
a country of particular concern in terms of its persecution of Christians. Moreover, the Barnabas Fund released a statement in October
2019 warning that individuals having a Holy Bible in Saudi Arabia
are at risk of being arrested (Gryboski 2019).

Christian leaders themselves have voiced their concern on the
plight of Christians throughout the Middle East region. Speaking on the fifth anniversary of Da'esh overrunning Christians on
the Nineveh Plain in northern Iraq, Chaldean Archbishop Bashar
Warda of Irbil warned that "with each successive cycle the number
of [Iraqi] Christians drop, till today we are at the point of extinction."
Archbishop Warda called on world leaders to act to end the discrimination and violence against Christians as well as members of other
minority religious populations in the region.

Similarly, in South Asia, countries such as India, Pakistan, and

Bangladesh are increasingly turning into "hot spots" in terms of the persecution of Christians. A 2019 report published by the Aid to the Church in Need, a pontifical foundation that provides relief to Christians around the world, concluded that Christians in this region of the world suffer from systematic harassment, violence, discrimination, abductions, forced conversions, and sex attacks (Hadro 2019). Pakistan is also a country of particular concern. According to Open Doors, Christians in Pakistan:

> ... continue to live in daily fear that they will be accused of blasphemy – which can carry a penalty of death. Additionally, radical Islamists seem to be gaining more political power, and the new ruling government must maintain good diplomatic relationships with some radical groups. Christians are largely regarded as second-class citizens, and conversion to Christianity from Islam carries a great deal of risk.
>
> Traditional, historical churches have relative freedom for worship and other activities; however, they are heavily monitored and have regularly been targeted for bomb attacks (for example, the Quetta bomb attack on Bethel Memorial Methodist Church in December 2017). Christian churches more active in outreach and youth work face stronger persecution in society.
>
> All Christians suffer from institutionalized discrimination, illustrated by the fact that occupations seen as low, dirty and derogatory are officially reserved for Christians. Many Christians are very poor, and some are victims of bonded labor. There are also many Christians belonging to the middle class, but their economic status doesn't save them from being marginalized or persecuted. The country's notorious blasphemy laws target religious minorities (including Muslim minorities), but affect the Christian minority in particular, not just the poor.[8]

Yet the so-called "Islamic groups" such as Daesh, al-Qaeda, and other affiliates that sympathize with their ideologies, blatantly disregard Muhammad's clear commandments in terms of treating Christians and religious minority populations with compassion and respect.

The broad treatment of Christians in the "Muslim world" today also contradicts Qur'anic passages, a significant issue considering that the Islamic holy text is viewed by Muslims as being the literal word of God. The Holy Qur'an refers to Jews, Christians, and

Sabaeans[9] as *ahl al-kitab*, or "People of the Book," a term denoting their possession of earlier books previously revealed by God. Here are additional Qur'anic passages that speak of Jews and Christians in a warm light:

> ... among the People of the Book, there is an upright community, reciting God's revelations in the watches of the night and prostrating (themselves in worship). They believe in God and the Last Day, and enjoin and promote what is right and good, and forbid and try to prevent evil, and hasten to do good deeds, as if competing with one another. Those are of the righteous ones. Whatever good they do, they will never be denied the reward of it; and God has full knowledge of the God-revering pious (Qur'an 3:113-115).

> And, behold, among the People of the Book are those who believe in God and what has been sent down to you, and what was sent down to them, those humbling themselves before God in reverence, not selling God's revelations for a trifling price. Such are those whose reward is with their Lord. God is swift at reckoning (Qur'an 3:199).

The Holy Qur'an also recognizes the special status of other monotheistic populations and traditions by considering Jews, Christians, and Sabeans as *dhimmi*,[10] or protected monotheistic minorities, thus permitting them to freely practice their faiths. Muslims are also required to defend these communities from both internal and external aggressions by people and communities seeking to inflict harm upon them.

Uri Avnery, the Israeli author, former member of Knesset, and founder of Gush Shalom Peace Movement, touched upon the *dhimmi* status in his discussion of "Muslim Spain,"[11] which he referred to as a "paradise for the Jews." He wrote: "... there has never been a Jewish Holocaust in the Muslim world. Even pogroms were extremely rare. Muhammad decreed that the 'Peoples of the Book' (Jews and Christians) be treated tolerantly, subject to conditions that were incomparably more liberal than those in contemporary Europe" (Avnery 2004).

These issues raise an important question – what can Muslim leaders do to ensure that freedom of religion reigns supreme within the borders of their states?

One answer is to strengthen Muhammad's vision of the *ummah* as one that is steeped in religious pluralism.

Before exploring Muhammad's relations with the "People of the Book," let us begin first by considering the meaning of "religious pluralism." Professor Diana Eck of The Pluralism Project at Harvard University is one of the foremost scholars on this sociological concept. Eck views religious pluralism as containing four primary elements.

The first element is the energetic engagement with religious diversity (Eck 2006). Religious pluralism is not simply diversity alone. Religious pluralism encourages sincere social interactions and the building of authentic relationships across perceived religious divides. Eck also clearly distinguishes religious pluralism and religious tolerance. Religious tolerance, she argues, allows people to stay in their isolated bubbles with little human interaction. Think, for example, about the last time that you tolerated a pattern of behavior of a family member, friend, or colleague. Is there something unacceptable that you find with that behavior? Is there something holding you back from really speaking your mind? Is there something a bit disengaging about tolerance in comparison to the kind of human engagement required by pluralism?

Tolerance, as viewed through the aforementioned example, allows "you to be you, and me to be me," but it does little to teach people that our well-being is dependent on the well-being of all members of society. Religious tolerance oftentimes reproduces old patterns of divisions and stereotypes primarily because tolerance is stand-offish. Because of these matters, Eck claims that religious tolerance "is too thin a foundation for a world of religious difference and proximity."

The second element of Eck's description of religious pluralism is the active seeking and understanding of the practices and beliefs of people from "other" religious populations. Religious pluralism calls for interreligious and intrareligious dialogue. Religious pluralism encourages human beings to enter into the places of worship, homes, and communities of the "other" to directly experience the norms and customs of religious populations. Religious pluralism calls on human beings to be comfortable with being uncomfortable, in the sense that experiencing something different and challenging can help individuals and communities grow in their knowledge, spirituality, and God consciousness.

With that said, the process of religious pluralism does not have to end up in what we may refer to as "*kumbaya* sessions."[12] Religious pluralism encourages us to have the difficult conversations about our beliefs, practices, and texts. We do not have to agree on everything. Rather, the process of religious pluralism seeks to foster knowledge and understanding in the hope that human beings are able to live peacefully with the vast array of differences found in the global human population.

Eck's third element of religious pluralism is the encounter of commitments. The new paradigm of religious pluralism, as Eck explains on The Pluralism Project website, "does not require us to leave our identities and our commitments behind… It means holding our deepest differences, even our religious differences, not in isolation, but in relationship to one another." By this she means that human beings and communities are able to be themselves while simultaneously committing themselves to shared principles that are also found in the religious and cultural traditions that fall outside of their immediate social circles.

Eck's fourth and final element of the new paradigm of pluralism is rooted in dialogue. The language of religious pluralism, she contends, is one of "give and take, criticism and self-criticism. Dialogue means both speaking and listening, and that process reveals both common understandings and real differences. Dialogue does not mean everyone at the 'table' will agree with one another. Pluralism involves the commitment to being at the table – with one's commitments."

Now that the concept of religious pluralism has been defined and distinguished from religious tolerance, let us see how Christian communities interacted with Prophet Muhammad and the early *ummah*.

The Christians of Najran

One of my favorite stories about Muhammad relates to his interactions with the Christians of Najran, a topic that I have covered in many speeches and lectures around the world. In February 2016,

I provided a talk for a dozen undergraduate and postgraduate students at Rice University in Houston, Texas. After the presentation I held a short question and answer session in which a postgraduate student challenged my claim that Muhammad promoted religious pluralism. The student claimed that the Covenants that Muhammad had entered into with Christians fostered religious tolerance instead of religious pluralism.

I asked the postgraduate student to consider the visit of the Christians of Najran to Muhammad's mosque, Al-Masjid al-Nabawi, in Medina. This visit is perhaps the most important and famous interaction between Christians and Muslim in world history. The event points to the kind of serious engagement in theological discussions and interreligious interactions in which Muslims and Christians commit themselves to common values while simultaneously maintaining their own religious beliefs. In other words, the encounter reinforces the distinction between religious pluralism and religious tolerance as described by Diana Eck.

A number of early Islamic manuscripts documented the interaction between the first Muslims and the Najran Christians. The story that these sources reveal unfolds something like this: Around June 631, Muhammad had sent Khalid ibn al-Walid to Najran to preach to Christians. The Muslim jurist Abu Ja'far Muhammad bin Jarir al-Tabari mentioned that al-Walid stayed with the Christians of Najran to teach them about Islamic beliefs and practices, and ultimately asked them to embrace Islam.[13]

Muhammad sent a follow-up letter, which was delivered by Mughira ibn Shu'ba, another of Muhammad's Companions. Ibn Shu'ba successfully persuaded the Najranis to accept Muhammad's invitation to visit Medina. The Najran delegation that traveled to visit Muhammad consisted of roughly sixty Christian learned-men, Bishop Ibn 'Alqamah, forty-five of his scholars, and fifteen assistants. There were two other notable men among the Christians of Najran – Abdul Maseeh, who was in charge of government affairs, and Al-Aiham as-Saiyid, who was in charge of educational and political affairs.

Muhammad is reported to have welcomed the Christian clergymen and diplomats of Najran to Al-Masjd al-Nabawi in Medina. This *masjid* is the second holiest site in the Islamic tradition and the second largest mosque in the world, behind Al-Masjid al-Haram in Mecca. Inside of the *masjid* the Christians and Muslims openly discussed matters of governance, politics, and theology.

The theological discussions were particularly interesting. Islamic sources record that the Muslims of Medina and the Christians of Najran shared common ground in their reverence of Jesus; they agreed that he was a messenger of God and a prophet that is distinguished among the prophets who came before him. The two delegations also agreed on Jesus' miraculous birth, ability to perform miracles, and title as the Messiah. While the Muslims and Christians saw eye-to-eye on these and other issues, they also agreed to disagree on the claim that Jesus is the Son of God, as believed and argued by the Najranis.

Despite their differing opinions on Christology,[14] if one idea can summarize their encounter, it is "mutual respect" achieved through the process of religious pluralism.

But the story does not end there.

Ibn Hisham, the scholar who edited the biography of Muhammad written by Ibn Ishaq, stated that the Christians of Najran cordially asked to leave the dialogue and proceed out of the Al-Masjid al-Nabawi in order to engage in their prayer. Ibn Hisham notes that Muhammad told the Christians that they were already in a house of God and that they were welcome to conduct their prayers inside of his *masjid*. The Christians of Najran accepted his offer.

Extending an invitation to the Christians to use his *masjid* as a place of worship is not merely religious tolerance – it is religious pluralism. Religious tolerance was achieved when Muhammad welcomed the Christians of Najran to Medina. Religious pluralism developed when the Christians and Muslims engaged in difficult conversations, agreed to disagree, and opened their doors to the "other" so that they could pray to God. Providing the Najranis a place to pray showed Muhammad's vision for the *ummah*, one that was anchored in freedom of religion and freedom of conscience, as well as hospitality and care for strangers and guests.

It is also worth pointing out that the Christian delegation did not accept Muhammad's invitation to embrace the Islamic faith. According to tradition, the Christians stated: "... we decided to leave you as you are and you leave us as we are. But send with us a man who can adjudicate things on our properties, because we accept you." Living with difference is an important part of religious pluralism. So too is the need to foster freedom of religion over the human desire to convert others to their own faith tradition.

Recalling Diana Eck, there are four elements to the process of religious pluralism: 1) the energetic engagement with religious diversity; 2) understanding across religious traditions; 3) the encounter of interreligious commitments; and 4) interreligious dialogue. Each of these characteristics is displayed in the meeting between the Christians of Najran and the Muslims of Medina. Muhammad engaged with the Christians in an interreligious theological discussion. The Christians and Muslims sought to understand the perspectives and experiences of the "other." Muhammad opened the doors of his place of worship to give Christians a space to pray. When the Christians of Najran left Medina, they did so with a covenant with Muhammad, who agreed to protect their life, liberty, and pursuit of happiness.

Perhaps it is an understatement to say that Muhammad merely tolerated the Christians of Najran. Religious tolerance is the absence of religious discrimination. Muhammad clearly embraced and welcomed the Otherness of Christians. That is religious pluralism.

The first *hijrah*

Another example of religious pluralism in the history of Christian and Muslim relations is the first *hijrah*, or migration, of the *ummah* in 615. At the time, the Meccan polytheists were persecuting Muhammad and his Companions because of the revolutionary ideas that came with the emergence of the Islamic faith and the revitalization of the monotheistic tradition. When the Prophet spoke out against the various gods that were being worshipped at the Ka'ba in Mecca, the Quraysh became actively hostile and began persecuting the early Muslim population. Muhammad was concerned that his community was on the brink of being wiped out, so he encouraged a group of men and women to seek asylum in Abyssinia. Some scholars, like W. Montgomery Watt, also argue that Muhammad encouraged the first Muslims to migrate to gain military support from the Christian rulers of Abyssinia, or to make Abyssinia the center of an alternative trade route out of the reach of Meccan merchants (Watt 1953: 66).

The earliest record of the *hijrah*, coming from Ibn Ishaq, suggests that Muhammad encouraged the migration to Abyssinia because he had learned that the Christian king in the city was a wise and just man that might be able to protect the early Muslim community from the wrath of the Quraysh leadership. Ibn Hisham and al-Tabari related Muhammad's words by writing: "If you were to go to Abyssinia (it would be better for you), for the king will not tolerate injustice and it is a friendly country, until such time as Allah shall relieve from you distress." Once they were in Abyssinia, the Muslims presented the Abyssinian king with an official letter from Muhammad, which read: "I have sent my cousin Ja'far to you, accompanied by a small number of Muslims; if he comes to you, receive them in hospitality."

The Muslims had the privilege of being in the presence of the King. The Christians of the Abyssinian royal court and the early members of the *ummah* engaged in a conversation on the similarities and differences between the Christian faith and the Islamic faith. On one occasion, a question was put to the Muslims: "What do you say concerning Jesus?" Ja'far responded: "... concerning Jesus we can only say what our Prophet has taught us: Jesus is the servant and messenger of God, the spirit and word of God, whom God entrusted to the Virgin Mary."

Pleased with what he had heard, the Abyssinian King decided to ask whether or not the Muslims had brought with them any of their revelations. Ja'far then read to him the chapter of the Holy Qur'an which explains the miraculous conception and birth of Jesus. Ibn Ishaq explained that after the King heard the passages from the Holy Qur'an he "... wept until his beard was wet and the bishops wept until their scrolls were wet."

The story does not end there. The King is said to have then picked up a stick from the ground. He turned to the Muslims and stated: "I swear, the difference between what we believe about Jesus, the Son of Mary, and what you have said is not greater than the width of this twig."

The first *hijrah* and the Muslims' interaction with the King of Abyssinia and the Christians in his royal court are poignant reminders of the promise and hope of Christian and Muslim relations. For starters, the event shows the compassionate spirit of Jesus and the Christian faith in the sense that the Christians of Abyssinia warmly embraced the Muslims to protect them from wrongdoing and harm. Second, the open and engaging discussion that they had on their theological traditions reveals the constructive nature of religious pluralism. The Christians and Muslims interacted with one another in a frank session of interreligious dialogue. While the two sides agreed to disagree on some core principles of their faith, they nevertheless left the setting with a more in-depth understanding of one another's communities as well as holy texts.

The Christian monks at Saint Catherine's Monastery

Resting in the library of Saint Catherine's Monastery at Mount Sinai in Egypt[15] is a document authorized by Prophet Muhammad that guarantees protection and other human rights to the Christians of this ancient community. The document, also referred to as the "Ashtiname of Muhammad" or the "Covenant of Prophet Muhammad with the Christian Monks of Mount Sinai," has received significant coverage in the news media in recent years. The popular CBS News television program – *60 Minutes* – visited Father Justin, a leader of Saint Catherine's, to explore the monastery's famous manuscript collection. In the *60 Minutes* clip, Father Justin pointed to the Ashtiname and stated: "These are precedence from Muhammad himself for toleration and peace among people of different faiths" (60 Minutes n.d.).

Protecting the Covenant with the Monks of Mount Sinai (see Appendix 3 for the complete text) and Saint Catherine's monastery itself has been a cause of concern in recent years, due largely to instability in Egypt and the rise of groups such as Da'esh in the region. In the aftermath of a string of attacks on Coptic Christians[16] in Egypt during the summer of 2013, I noticed that some Muslims had betrayed the Prophet's message of peace and goodwill to the Christian community at Saint Catherine's monastery. A number of major news websites across the world reported in April 2017 that Da'esh gunmen opened fire on Egyptian police officers near the checkpoint of the monastery, killing one officer and wounding four others (Khoury 2017). Also in April 2017, a series of deadly bombings rocked two Coptic churches, killing more than 40 people and injuring dozens of others. Both attacks occurred on Palm Sunday – one of the holiest days in the Christian calendar. Da'esh, or the Islamic State of Iraq and Syria (otherwise known as ISIS), claimed responsibility for the attacks (Blumberg 2017).

In response to this attack and others on the Christian population across the Middle East, Azeem Ibrahim, a scholar at the Strategic Studies Institute at the U.S. Army War College, wrote an opinion piece for the website Foreign Policy. According to Ibrahim, Da'esh's action "were not only horrific but also clearly and universally recognized as blasphemy" (Ibrahim 2017). What Ibrahim meant by blasphemy is that attacking Christians is inherently against the teachings of Muhammad as they concern the treatment of religious minority populations such as Christians.

Moreover, in June 2014, a retired Egyptian Army general, Ahmed Ragai Attiya, said he had filed a court order which would push for the demolition of Saint Catherine's monastery. General Attiya called for the destruction of the monastery's multiple churches, monk cells, gardens, and other historic places of interest and significance. Attiya leveled a host of accusations against the monks of Saint Catherine's, alleging that they had changed the names of landmarks in the area, and tried to hide an underground water source known as "Moses's well." If the demolition were to occur, monks would be displaced, and the Covenant of Prophet Muhammad would be endangered and potentially lost forever.

The Covenant has received additional attention in academic circles, with questions circling around its history and authenticity. The original covenant was moved from Saint Catherine's monastery by Sultan Selim I of the Ottoman Empire in 1517, and today its replica can be seen in the Topkapi Museum in Istanbul.[17] When Sultan Selim took the document to Topkapi, he renewed its terms and gave the resident monks in the Sinai a copy (Ibrahim 2019). This copy is reportedly still at the monastery, as claimed in the *60 Minutes* piece.

The Covenant of Prophet Muhammad with the Christian Monks of Mount Sinai is one of many covenants said to be authorized by Muhammad himself. Unknown to many Christians and Muslims around the world, the Covenants are a set of documents outlining Muhammad's vision for the *ummah*.

John Andrew Morrow's book, *The Covenants of the Prophet Muhammad with the Christians of the World*, offers critical insight into these "treaties." He even encourages scholars to use the Covenants as a third foundational source of the *sharia*, or "Islamic law," in addition to the Holy Qur'an and *Hadith*.

Morrow's book provides a detailed account of Muhammad's character and conduct as seen through his lifelong interactions with Christian hermits, monks, priests, communities, and nations. Morrow states that these experiences confirm that Muhammad had "confidence in his ability to count on the spiritual solidarity of the 'People of the Book.'" The Prophet, Morrow noted, did not create a "new religion" that combined Judeo-Christian beliefs and practices together with pagan traditions. As far as Muslims are concerned, Muhammad "purified, perfected, and completed the primordial monotheistic tradition of Adam, Abraham, Moses, and Jesus. The issue, then, is not of borrowing, but rather of belonging, reviving, revitalizing, and renewing" (Morrow 2013: 13).

The Covenant of Prophet Muhammad with the Monks of Mount Sinai is a type of medicine to cure the world of religious intolerance. In the Covenant the Prophet championed human rights including freedom of worship, freedom of conscience, and the right to protection during a time of war, among other privileges. Here is passage from the covenant, as translated by John Andrew Morrow:

> This covenant was written by Muhammad, the son of 'Abd Allah, the proclaimer and warner, trusted to protect Allah's creations, in order that people may raise no claim against Allah after [the advent of] His Messengers for Allah is Almighty, Wise.
>
> He has written it for the members of his religion and to all those who profess the Christian religion in East and West, near or far, Arabs or non-Arabs, known or unknown, as a covenant of protection. If anyone breaks the covenant herein proclaimed, or contravenes or

transgresses its commands, he has broken the Covenant of Allah, breaks his bond, makes a mockery of his religion, deserves the curse [of Allah], whether he is a sultan or another among the believing Muslims.

If a monk or pilgrim seeks protection, in mountain or valley, in a cave or in tilled fields, in the plain, in the desert, or in a church, I am behind them, defending them from every enemy; I, my helpers, all the members of my religion, and all my followers, for they [the monks and the pilgrims] are my proteges and my subjects (Morrow 2015:13-14).

The Covenant between Muhammad, his Companions, and the Christians of Mount Sinai championed universal peace and harmony between Muslims and Christians. The text clearly states that Muhammad is "behind [Christians], defending them from every enemy." Bishops and monks, as noted in the document, shall not be hindered in their religious practices or pilgrimages, and that churches shall not be destroyed.

Morrow captures the spirit of the Covenant with the Christian Monks of Mount Sinai as being:

... a clear rejection of classism, elitism, and racism... all [people] are equal before God for whom the most important thing is not language, skin color, social status or class position, which exclude others, but rather the degree of piety, humanity, love for others (which includes not only human beings but the entire natural order), sincerity of faith, the acceptance of His Commandments, and complete certainty as to the special place occupied by His Prophets, Messengers, and Imams (Morrow 2013:89).

It is also worth noting that this Covenant made it clear that anyone who "breaks the covenant herein proclaimed, or contravenes or transgresses its commands ... has broken the Covenant of Allah, breaks his bond, makes a mockery of his religion, deserves the curse [of God], whether he is a sultan or another among the believing Muslims."

The idea that Prophet Muhammad was "anti-Christian" is further dispelled by turning to his Covenant with the Christians of

Persia. In this agreement, the Prophet made it clear that he had no interest in converting Persians to the Islamic faith. He proclaimed: "No Christian shall be brought by force to confess Islam." Instead of aggressively encouraging Christians to accept the Muslim faith, Muhammad hoped that Muslims would show Christians "the arm of mercy and kindness" by protecting them from "the exactions of oppressors." If he had thought that Christians were inferior, would the Prophet have gone to such lengths to support them and care for their well-being?

It is also worth considering Prophet Muhammad's views on Muslims who call Christians cruel names or condemn them to the hellfire. Muhammad explicitly laid out the consequences of disrespecting Christians: "He who wrongs a [Christian] will have myself as his accuser on the Day of Judgment" (Al-Bukhari). This passage mirrors a Qur'anic verse that reads: "Those who believe (i.e. professing to be Muslims), or those who declare Judaism, or the Christians or the Sabaeans (or those of some other faith) whoever truly believes in God and the Last Day and does good, righteous deeds, surely their reward is with their Lord, and they will have no fear, nor will they grieve" (Qur'an 2:62). The Prophet made it clear: Muslims are not to judge others and Christians will have their reward of heaven if they display faith, piety, and good actions.

Across all the Covenants, Muhammad stated that Christians were allowed to build and repair churches, that Christian women should be allowed to pray in churches, and that Christian priests were able to maintain their roles as community leaders. Muhammad made it obligatory for all Muslims to abide by his commandments both at the present-time and in the future.

As a whole, the Covenants of Muhammad with the Christians of his time uniformly command Muslims to protect peaceful Christian communities, in essence, to energetically engage with them to ensure that all of their practical and spiritual needs are met. That, again, is religious pluralism, rather than religious tolerance.

While Muhammad was an Arab, it is certainly worth noting that Arabs are not the only Muslim leaders who welcomed the presence of Jews and Christians in the *ummah*. Consider, for instance, the Ottoman Empire. The official status of Jews and Christians under the Ottoman Empire was *ahl al-kitab*, or "People of the Book," as mandated by the Holy Qur'an. As a result, these two minority populations were given official state protection, or *ahl al-dhimmi*. Both communities were afforded a degree of legal autonomy and authority and the Ottoman government responded to needs with various arrangements depending on time and location.

The Turkish term *millet* during the Ottoman Empire years referred to communities based on their religious identifications. Writing for Oxford Bibliographies, scholar Efrat Aviv describes *millet* system in the Ottoman Empire in the following manner:

> In the Qur'an, millet frequently refers to the "*millat* Ibrahim," or religion of Abraham … There are also references to millet as "religion, confession, or rite" from 1158 to 1833 in various internal and international communications, mainly between the Ottoman Empire and non-Muslim empires. Occasionally, millet was translated in the West as "sovereign nations," especially in terms of rebellion. Commonly, millet was defined as a "religious community"… the Ottomans used it to give minority religious communities within their Empire limited power to regulate their own affairs, under the overall supremacy of the Ottoman administration … The Ottomans allowed the "religions of the book" to be organized in millets: the Orthodox Christians or Rums, the Armenians, and the Jews. Non-Muslims had to be part of a millet to be considered citizens of the empire (Aviv 2016).

Following Aviv, scholars Karen Barkey and George Gavrilis argued that the *millet* system was a successful example of the Ottoman state giving autonomy to Jews and Christians. Barkey and Gavrilis concluded that the Ottoman rulers recognized the diversity of religious and ethnic communities within the empire, and that this diversity could not and should not be assimilated into an overarching principles of "sameness" (Barkey and Gavrilis 2015: 24).

The privileges granted to Jews and Christians under Ottoman rule were not always guaranteed to minorities in Europe, where Jews and Muslims were often persecuted or held back due to religious prejudice (Baraz 2010: 1). With that said, it is important to note that Jews and Christians did not enjoy complete freedom in Ottoman territories. These two populations were required to pay the *jizya*, or special tax on minorities. Further, while Jews and Christians were allowed to hold certain high ranking positions in the government and elsewhere in society, such as financial advisers or physicians, they were always required to hold only those positions subordinate to their Muslim counterparts (Baraz 2010: 1). It should be noted here that in return for *jizya*, non-Muslims were exempt from other burdens like military service (which gave them the *dhimmi*, i.e. "the protected," status) or other taxes like *zakat* or *sadaqa al-fitr*, which Muslims were required to pay.

The culture of encounter

In the 7th century, Muhammad prophesized that a time would come when nothing would remain of Islam but its name, and nothing of the Qur'an or *Hadith* but its word. In these days, as Kashif Chaudhry noted, the true spiritual essence of the Islamic faith would be lost, and religion, for the most part, would be reduced to a ritualistic compulsion (Chaudhry 2016). Muhammad, as Chaudry claims, described how terrorist groups such as Daesh or al-Qaeda would try to hijack the Islamic faith by committing heinous deeds. The Prophet even classified these kind of people as "the worst of the creation."

Radical interpretations of religion like those of Daesh and al-Qaeda, according to Pope Francis, is a "plague on humanity." To counter exclusive, harmful, and even violent interpretations of religion, the Pope calls on human beings to engage in interreligious dialogue and cross-faith solidarity as ways to counter fundamentalist interpretations of religion.

Meeting with members of the Argentine Institute for Interreligious Dialogue in November 2019, Francis said that in today's precarious world, "dialogue among religions is not a weakness. It finds its reason for being in the dialogue of God with humanity" (Arocho Esteves 2019). The Pope's encouraging words reflect the way that God speaks about humanity in the Biblical tradition. God uses the plural pronouns of "us" to refer to the population of human beings.

Pope Francis has served as a key figure in the global movement to foster stronger relations between Christians and Muslims. On

February 4th, 2019, he, alongside Sheikh Ahmed El-Tayeb,[18] signed "A Document on Human Fraternity for World Peace and Living Together" in Abu Dhabi, United Arab Emirates (See Appendix 5 for the full text). The Document reads:

> We, who believe in God and in the final meeting with him and his judgment, on the basis of our religious and moral responsibility, and through this document, call upon ourselves, upon the leaders of the world as well as the architects of international policy and world economy, to work strenuously to spread the culture of tolerance and of living together in peace.

The intention of the document, Francis explained, was to adopt a "culture of dialogue and encounter" while respecting each other's unique identities. The Pope encouraged his concept of the "culture of encounter" in a morning mediation in the chapel of the *Domus Sanctae Marthae* in September 2016:

> An invitation to work for "the culture of encounter," in a simple way, "as Jesus did": not just seeing, but looking; not just hearing, but listening; not just passing people by, but stopping with them; not just saying "what a shame, poor people!", but allowing yourself to be moved with compassion; "and then to draw near, to touch and to say: 'Do not weep' and to give at least a drop of life' (Pope Francis 2016).

In general, Pope Francis hopes that the culture of encounter captures "the idea of reaching out, fostering dialogue and friendship even outside the usual circles, and making a special point of encountering people who are neglected and ignored by the wider world" (Allen Jr. 2013).

This powerful image of Christian and Muslim relations echoes not only the fraternity developed between Muhammad and the Christians of his time, but also Saint Francis of Assisi's mission to Egyptian Sultan Malek al-Kamil 800 years ago, an encounter that Pope Francis has touched upon before in his global addresses.

In 1219, Saint Francis and Sultan al-Kamil met during a flashpoint in the long history of the Crusades, specifically, the Fifth Crusade.[19] Saint Francis ventured into enemy lines to meet with the al-Kamil in Damietta, Egypt, knowing full well that the risk could lead to his death or imprisonment. It is arguably the first ever meeting of its kind. Never before had two such powerful leaders from two different religious backgrounds met together in the spirit of peace and understanding (Kenny 2019). Allyson Kenny, a producer of Salt and Light Television,[20] explains the encounter in a vibrant manner:

> The backdrop of the visit was the Fifth Crusade and the siege of the Egyptian city of Damietta, located along a tributary of the Nile River and situated near the southern coast of the Mediterranean Sea. Though Francis had seen war between city-states before in his native Italy, nothing had prepared him for the sight of carnage on this scale. Obstinate Christian leaders refused to accept generous offers of truce and monetary reward from Muslim leaders; a fifth of the Christian army died of typhus in the squalid camps along the Nile while the siege dragged on. Saracen soldiers caught by Crusaders were mutilated; in revenge, Muslim galleys along the river hurled fire and tar at the Christian siege forces. When they disembarked, the Saracens were known to impale any women and children from the camp that got in their way.
>
> So naturally, when Francis and his companion, Illuminatus (one of his brothers with a rudimentary knowledge of Arabic), left the Christian camp for al-Kamil's headquarters, it seemed nothing short of a suicide mission. That they even made it to appear before the Sultan at all speaks to our respective religious tradition's shared heritage of consecrating oneself to the Divine. Al-Kamil's guards likely mistook Francis and Illuminatus for Holy Men in the same vein as Muslim Sufis, who wore a simple belted tunic similar to the type we still see Franciscans wearing today. They may also have expected that these men of faith were emissaries sent to continue negotiations on behalf of the Christian army.
>
> Al-Malik al-Kamil was widely known as a pious and devout man. The nephew of the infamous Saladin, he received an excellent military education but was known to prefer the discipline of prayer to the sword. A strong believer in the One God, al-Kamil summoned his advisers to listen as Francis spoke of the story of salvation history, its

culmination in the person of Jesus Christ, and a plea in the name of God for peace between the warring factions.

Perhaps unsurprisingly given his character, al-Kamil knew holiness when he saw it. Against the advice of his advisers – who recommended killing Francis, the usual punishment for Christians in a Muslim land who, though allowed to practice their faith, were legally subject to capital punishment should they try to preach conversion away from Islam – he spared Francis, even inviting him to spend a week in his residence as an esteemed guest.

While we know nothing of the content of the conversations between Francis and the Sultan, we do know that Francis and Illuminatus left a week later, untouched and unharmed. They were gifted ample provisions for their return journey, even refusing an offer of precious gifts (which impressed al-Kamil even further). They were not, however, unchanged.

Francis had left for Damietta with martyrdom on his mind; in a way, he truly hoped the Sultan would have him executed, so he could die what he deemed a glorious, saintly death. Instead, in the Crusader's filthy camp, he contracted the trachoma infection that would eventually leave him nearly blind and in constant pain for the rest of his life. With eyes oozing, irritated, and inflamed, it was a different kind of martyrdom than the one he envisioned but martyrdom nonetheless. The dialogue with al-Kamil seems to have changed Francis' heart, too, challenging his assumptions about someone who had once seemed so "other." Perhaps it was Francis, not al-Kamil, that needed to be "converted" after all.

Other details of the encounter between Saint Francis and Sultan al-Kamil provide hope for constructive and enriching relations between Christians and Muslims. It is said that Francis greeted the Sultan with the greeting, "May the Lord give you peace," a phrase that is clearly similar in nature to the traditional Islamic greeting of, *as-salamu alaikum,* or peace be upon you. Francis was able to preach the Gospel in front of al-Kamil's court, but the Sultan was not offended and certainly did not condemn the Saint on the charges of blasphemy or heresy. Upon his departure from Damietta, Francis was gifted by Sultan al-Kamil with a range of precious presents, but

Francis refused to accept them because he had taken a vow of poverty years earlier. The Sultan was said to have been speechless. Yet, Francis ended up accepting one gift – an ivory horn – which today is on display in Assisi, Italy.

The "culture of encounter" that Pope Francis encouraged and Saint Francis lived is the same kind of practice that Muhammad advocated for nearly 1,400 years ago. This culture is much more than mere talk. It is also much more than a theory. It is a necessary and active process that requires human beings to be fearless in the ways that they interact with humanity. May we embrace the culture of encounter by denouncing exclusion and isolation and embracing inclusion and integration. Amen.

Chapter Two

Civic Nation State Building

Philip K. Hitti, the 20th century Christian scholar of Arab Studies, praised Muhammad for his ability to form an unprecedented kind of nation state in such a short period of time. Hitti stated: "Within a brief span of mortal life, Muhammad called forth of unpromising material, a nation, never welded before; in a country that was hitherto but a geographical expression; he established a religion which in vast areas surpassed Christianity and Judaism, and laid the basis of an empire that was soon to embrace within its far flung boundaries the fairest provinces in the civilized world" (Hitti 1970: 3-4).[21]

The unprecedented type of nation that Hitti was referring to was a civic nation state, another key feature of Muhammad's vision for the *ummah*. A civic nation state can be defined as "a community of equal, rights-bearing citizens, united in patriotic attachment to a shared set of political practices and values" (Ignatieff 1993: 6). Civic nation states envision "'one people' with a common sense of 'we,' but not in the sense that 'we' derives from a particular ethnicity or religion" (Considine 2016a: 13). Members of a civic nation state are citizens who are bounded by a set of laws that give no preference to any particular religious, ethnic, or racial group. A civic nation state "allows individuals to define the national community rather than having the national community define the individual" (ibid.). Furthermore, people living in a civic nation state are unified by their political rights as outlined in a constitution and their free will as individuals to "opt in" to in terms of belonging to the nation.

The notion of a civic nation state is juxtaposed with the idea of an ethnic nation state or racial nation state. A nation steeped in ethnicity is a community in which ancestry, marriage, and blood define a person's worth and sense of belonging to a given nation. In this sense an ethnic or racial nation state "is an exclusive nation because it places emphasis on historical experiences and the resulting phenotypes that outline the boundary of the 'natives'" (Considine 2016a: 13). A classic example of an ethnic or racial nation state is the Nazi regime of Germany during the 1930s and 1940s. Under the Third Reich and Adolf Hitler's authoritarian rule, membership into the German nation state was predicated on ethnicity and race and these two features alone. All human beings that were considered inferior or from "impure" ethnicities or races were excluded from equal rights and, at worst, placed into labor camps and eventual extermination.

The depth of Muhammad's preference for a civic nation state can be found in the Constitution of Medina (see Appendix 1), an agreement that he made with a diverse group of people to ensure that no single group in Medina would be able to seize control of the power dynamics in society. Also referred to as the Medina Charter or the *Ummah* Document, the Constitution of Medina established equal rights between Jews, Muslims, pagans, and perhaps even a handful of Christians living under Muslim-rule, or an "Islamic state." The document is believed to be one of the first – if not the first – constitution in world history to guarantee freedom of religion and freedom of conscience to all members of a given nation state.

The Constitution of Medina was formed shortly after the second *hijrah*, or migration of the *ummah*. Around 622, Muhammad and his followers moved north to Medina, which was Yathrib before the coming of the Islamic faith, as a way to escape persecution in Mecca, but also to mediate the various disputes between the clans and diverse people from which the city suffered. In Medina, the Arab and Jewish inhabitants had been fighting one another for hundreds of years. Muhammad, known as a reliable man who could be trusted to offer objective and fair judgments in times of conflict, was chosen to forge a lasting peace that could bring hope for all residents of Medina.

Muhammad and the *ummah*'s connection with the Jewish people of Medina was a natural connection. In a sense, the Muslims and

Jews, as well as the Christians of Medina, were natural allies. The Holy Qur'an says that the Jews are God's chosen people: "We did for sure grant to the Children of Israel the book, and the authority to judge (by the Book), and Prophethood; and We provided them with pure, wholesome things, and exalted them above all other peoples (of their time)" (Qur'an 45:16).

As Muhammad's leadership cemented and the tension in Medina settled down, the Prophet shifted his aims to an ambitious project – unite the diverse groups residing in the city by creating a confederation of peoples that would be governed by a constitution. To achieve his goal, Muhammad entered into an agreement with the Medinese tribes that is known as the Constitution of Medina. Scholars believe that the Constitution of Medina appears to be of documentary quality and early Muslim historians also accepted the agreement's authenticity and value.

In regards to Judaism specifically, the Constitution of Medina singled out Jews who, Muhammad agreed in Article 25, "shall be considered one political community (the *ummah*) along with the believers (i.e. the Muslims) – for the Jews their religion, and for the Muslim theirs, be one client or patron." This article is clear in that it grants Jews both freedom of religion and freedom of conscience. The Constitution of Medina adds in Article 16: "And that those who will obey us among the Jews, will have help and equality. Neither shall they be oppressed nor will any help be given against them."

Article 44 of the Constitution went even further by stating: "And they (i.e., Jews and Muslims) shall have each other's help in the event of any one invading Yathrib (Medina)." Moreover, even strangers living in the *ummah*, as outlined in the Constitution, were to be treated with special consideration and on the same ground as their protectors. These passages clearly confirm the idea that the health of the Medinan society is dependent on the well-being of all populations present in the city, and that the Medinese are effectively one body that should be ready and willing to defend the interest of all members of society. Muhammad's Constitution helped to actualize the idea of a sole community made up of diverse people living under one government and ultimately one creator, God.

According to Ira M. Lapidus, Muhammad, as head of the Med-inese state, separated religious matters from political matters, an action that is widely regarded as a fundamental component of any civic nation. In doing so, the Prophet set a precedent that was adopted by future generations of the *ummah*. Lapidus explains that the leaders of the *ummah* developed distinct spheres of influence for religious and political matters respectively. From the middle of the tenth-century onwards, many "Muslim empires" had passed power into the hands of generals, administrators, governors, and local provincial lords, some of whom were Christian. Governments in "Islamic lands," Lapidus claims, were essentially secular regimes without any intrinsic religious character, although they were officially loyal to the Islamic faith and committed to its defense.[22]

The Constitution of Medina, according to John Andrew Morrow, created a nation state out of "a unique system which had never existed before and which has never been since despite honest efforts to emulate it" (Morrow 2013: 32). Here is how Morrow described the kind of nation envisioned by Muhammad in the Constitution itself:

> Identity and loyalty were no longer to be based on family, tribe, kin-ship, or even religion: the overriding identity was membership in the *ummah* of Muhammad. The Constitution of Medina decreed that the citizens of the Islamic state were one and indivisible regardless of religion. Be they heathen, People of the Book, or Muslims, all those who were subject to the Constitution belonged to the same *ummah*. In doing so, he created a tolerant, pluralistic government which protected religious freedom.

Morrow's description of Muhammad's vision for the *ummah* mirrors a statement that Jawaharlal Nehru, the first President of the Indian National Congress and the first prime minister of India, made centuries later: "Like the founders of some other religions, Moham-mad was a rebel against many of the existing social customs. The religion he preached, by its simplicity and directness and its flavor of democracy and equality, appealed to the masses."

The Covenant with the Christian Monks of Mount Sinai also demonstrates Muhammad's preference for civic nation state building rather than ethnic or racial nation state building. In this Covenant, the Prophet, as the head of a state with an agreed upon constitution, guaranteed protection to minority populations in the "East and West, near or far, Arabs or non-Arabs, known or unknown." He added in this covenant: "I am behind them, defending them from every enemy... There shall be no compulsion or constraint against them [in any matter]." These words echo a similar passage in the Holy Qur'an: "There is no compulsion in the religion. The right way stands there clearly distinguished from the false" (Qur'an 2:256).

What the Constitution of Medina and the Covenant with the Christian Monks of Mount Sinai teach us is that the *ummah*, as envisioned by Muhammad, is one that is anti-hierarchical and non-centralist in terms of governance; it was meant to be a confederation of religious groupings rather than a space for Muslims alone (Considine 2016a: 15). A person's rights in the *ummah* did not derive from kinship or ethnic ties or the feeling that a person is responsible for – and committed to – their tribe or ethnicity alone. Instead, rights in the *ummah* rested on the ability of citizens to get a "fair hearing" for their views and "fair protection of their interests" (Barry 1993: 2). Furthermore, according to Frederick M. Denny, a scholar of the early years of the *ummah*, kinship was not the main binding tie of the "Muslim nation." Monotheism, however, was of greater importance. For Denny, the *ummah* is a kind of "super tribe" made up of people of various religious backgrounds that were united by God and Muhammad as the main authority of the nation (Denny 1977).

Muhammad's ideas in terms of incorporating religious, ethnic, and racial minorities is similar to the words used in the Declaration of the Rights of Man and of the Citizen, a document passed in 1789 by the National Constituent Assembly of the French republic. Article VI of the Declaration states that all citizens of France are legally protected and "eligible to all honors, places, and employments, according to their different abilities without any other distinction than that created by their virtues and talents."

Finally, Muhammad insisted that the government of the *ummah* is not the property of any particular religious, ethnic, or racial group. His "Islamic state" gave no preference to one or more groups, meaning that he did not devalue people based on their ethnicity, religion, or even their culture. According to Anna Stilz, this kind of nation is one that emphasizes "neutrality" which holds that "the state should pursue no policies that have the end result that one way of life is advantaged, favored, or assisted in ways others are not" (Stilz 2009: 265).

Muhammad's vision and "American values"

Although they are typically seen to be total opposites, the vision of Muhammad and the U.S. Founding Fathers shares common characteristics that can be explored through various historical texts. Muhammad and the U.S. Founding Fathers shared an interest in protecting people as equal members of society regardless of their religion, ethnicity, race.[23] Muhammad, for example, received revelations from God, who directed him to celebrate diversity and cherish it as a staple of his nation state. Muhammad's encounter with the word of God, the Holy Qur'an, would include verses like the following, which unequivocally states: "O humankind! Surely We have created you from a single (pair of) male and female, and made you into tribes and families so that you may know one another" (Qur'an 49:13). Here are several other Qur'anic passages on the importance of embracing diversity:

> "And among His signs is that He created you from earth, and (since) then, you have grown into a human population scattered widely" (Qur'an 30:20).
>
> "Among His signs is the creation of the heavens and the earth, and the diversity of your languages and colors. Surely in this are signs for people who have knowledge (of facts in creation, and who are free of prejudices)" (Qur'an 30:22).
>
> "Do you not see that God sends down water from the sky? Then We bring forth with it produce of various colors (shapes and tastes) and in the mountains are streaks of white and red, of various colors (due to the flora of the variety of stone and rock), as well as raven-black" (Qur'an 35:27).

The U.S. Founding Fathers had a similar vision in terms of embracing diversity in its many forms. On July 4th, 1776, the Second Continental Congress gathered in Philadelphia, Pennsylvania to write the Declaration of Independence, which stated the principles of the U.S. government and declared that the thirteen original colonies were independent sovereign states, no longer under the rule of King George III of the United Kingdom of Great Britain. The second paragraph of the Declaration states that "[Americans] hold these truths to be self-evident, that all men are created equal, that they are endowed by their Creator with certain unalienable Rights, that among these are Life, Liberty and the pursuit of Happiness."

When the U.S. Constitution was ratified in 1787, the Founding Fathers also put into practice the First Amendment which reads: "Congress shall make no law respecting an establishment of religion, or prohibiting the free exercise thereof; or abridging the freedom of speech...," which suggests that, by law, no single group is to be treated in a superior manner in the United States. In essence, every citizen of the country is granted the human rights of freedom of religion, freedom of conscience, and freedom of speech.[24]

George Washington, one of the most important Founding Fathers, adopted a similar approach to nation state building as Prophet Muhammad. Washington wrote in a 1783 letter to a friend that "the bosom of America is open to receive... the oppressed and persecuted of all nations and religions, whom [U.S. citizens] shall welcome to a participation of all [their] rights and privileges... They may be [Muslims], Jews, or Christians of any sect."[25] Muhammad's embrace of the Jewish population of Medina is similar to the language that Washington used in another letter dated to 1783. Writing to the Jewish community of Newport, Rhode Island, Washington noted that "the children of the stock of Abraham, who dwell in this land, [will] continue to merit and enjoy the goodwill of their inhabitants." These tributes to Jews by Muhammad and Washington are important reminders for Muslims worldwide and Americans to continue their struggle against the stain of anti-Semitism.

The Founding Fathers also had a track record of engaging with the so-called "Muslim world." Their first official diplomatic interaction occurred at the twilight of the Revolutionary period when the United States government made contact with the Barbary States,[26] which, at the time, were autonomous provinces of the Ottoman Empire on the coast of North Africa (Considine 2019: 55). The Founding Fathers agreed to the Treaty of Peace and Friendship (see Appendix 4) in 1787 with Mohammed ibn Abdullah, the Sultan of Morocco. The 1787 treaty granted U.S. trading vessels the freedom to navigate around the North African coast for the purpose of initiating commerce. Years later, in 1796, the treaty was reaffirmed with the signing of the Treaty of Peace and Friendship between the United States of America and the Bey and Subjects of Tripoli of Barbary (see Appendix 3). Article 11 of the 1796 treaty stated, "The United States of America is not in any sense founded on the Christian religion, as it has in itself no character or enmity against the laws, religion, or tranquility of [Muslims], and as the said States never have entered into any war or act of hostility against any Muslim nation, it is declared by the parties that no pretext arising from religious opinions shall ever produce an interruption of the harmony existing between two countries."

Although he was not a Founding Father, the American author, Washington Irving, was no doubt inspired by their thirst for knowledge. Irving is recognized as being the first U.S. citizen to write a biography of Prophet Muhammad. After living in the Alhambra[27] and subsequently writing several books on the achievements of "Muslim Spain," Irving decided to write *The Life of Mahomet*. Here is a passage from the book:

> [Muhammad's] deportment, in general, was calm and equable ... he is said to have possessed a smile of captivating sweetness ... in his excited and enthusiastic moments there was a glow and radiance in his countenance, which his disciples magnified into the supernatural light of prophecy. His intellectual qualities were undoubtedly of an extraordinary kind ... In his private dealings he was just. He treated friends and strangers, the rich and poor, the powerful and the weak, with equity, and was beloved by the common people for the affability with which he received them, and listened to their complaints ... he was kind and tolerant" (Irving 1859: 192-193).

A similar kind of appreciation for Prophet Muhammad was offered decades earlier by Benjamin Franklin, another Founding Father of the United States of America. Franklin's respect for Muhammad's example came forth in 1763 and 1764 following several attacks on Native Americans by the Paxton Boys, a frontiersmen militia group of Ulster Protestant immigrants from Scotland. One notable attack, referred to as the Conestoga Massacre, saw the Paxton boys slaughter twenty innocent and defenseless Susquehannock (Contestoga) Native Americas, near Lancaster, Pennsylvania. The Paxton Boys accused the Susquehannock of conspiring with other Native Americans against them.

In his text *A Narrative of the Late Massacres in Lancaster County, of a Number of Indians, Friends of this Province, By Persons Unknown*, Franklin condemned the actions of the Ulster Protestants from Scotland by citing Prophet Muhammad's merciful approach towards enemies and combatants in war. Franklin stated:

> As for the Turks[28], it is recorded in the Life of Mahomet, the founder of their religion, that Khaled, one of his captains, having divided a number of prisoners between himself and those that were with him, he commanded the hands of his own prisoners to be tied behind them, and then, in a most cruel and brutal manner, put them to the sword; but he could not prevail on his men to massacre their captives, because in fight they had laid down their arms, submitted, and demanded protection. Mahomet (i.e. Prophet Muhammad), when the account was brought to him, applauded the men for their humanity; but said to Khaled, with great indignation, "O Khaled, thou butcher, cease to molest me with thy wickedness. If thou possessedst a heap of gold as large as Mount Obod, and shouldst expend it all in God's cause, thy merit would not efface the guilt incurred by the murder of the meanest of those poor captives (Franklin 1856: 73-74).

Franklin, who is said to have never subscribed himself to any particular faith or religious tradition, was also a proponent of freedom of religion and freedom of conscience, just like Muhammad was in the 7th century. Around 1739, Franklin helped the city of Philadelphia to raise money for a new religious building to be built for the city's population. As Franklin wrote in his diary, the house of worship was "expressly for the use of any preacher of any religious persuasion who might desire to say something to the people at Philadelphia: the design in building not being to accommodate any particular sect, but the inhabitants in general; so that even if the Mufti[29] of Constantinople were to send a missionary to preach Mohammedanism to us, he would find a pulpit at his service" (Franklin 1986: 87-88).

CHAPTER THREE

ANTI-RACISM

"Globally, racial equality is under attack."

Tendayi Achiume, the United Nations Special Rapporteur on contemporary forms of racism, racial discrimination, xenophobia, and related intolerance, made the above statement in front of the United Nations General Assembly in a commemoration for the International Day for the Elimination of Racial Discrimination in March 2019.[30] Achiume went on to explain: "From crowds of youths marching to neo-Nazi chants in Charlottesville, Warsaw and Berlin, to the racist and xenophobic attitudes of politicians in the highest levels of office worldwide [...] the assault on the human dignity of millions around the world has reached alarming proportions."

The United Nations press release of the commemoration added, "extremism and systemic racial exclusion threatened not only the specific groups they targeted, but also the very political and legal foundations of states... [We call] on people to consider how they could better promote tolerance, inclusion, and respect for diversity... messages of hatred and the concept of 'us' and 'them' must be eliminated."

While it is clear that racial inequality and racism pose alarming challenges to humanity, less attention appears to be given to the potential solutions that can solve these pressing concerns. What, then, can human beings do to combat racial inequality and racism?

One option is to follow Muhammad, who is regarded by some as the world's first anti-racist.

Before examining Muhammad's views on anti-racism, let us first come to an understanding over the definition of racism and racist. According to the Merriam-Webster Dictionary, racism is "a belief that race is the primary determinant of human traits and capacities and that racial differences produce an inherent superiority of a particular race." Ibram X. Kendi, author of *How to Be an Anti-racist*, writes that a racist is therefore someone "who is supporting a racist policy through their actions or inaction of expressing a racist idea."

Non-racism, on the other hand, is the "passive rejection, opposition, and disassociation from behaviors, discourses, and ideologies that are considered racist" (King 2016: 63). Non-racism signifies neutrality, but as Kendi points out again, "there is no neutrality in the racism struggle. The opposite of racist isn't 'not racist.' It is 'anti-racist.' ... One either endorses the idea of a racial hierarchy as a racist or racial equality as an antiracist" (Taylor 2019).

An anti-racist, as Kendi elaborates, is one "who is supporting an antiracist policy through their actions or expressing an antiracist idea" (Ruiz 2019). For him, being antiracist means "moving beyond the 'not racist' defense and instead embracing and articulating decidedly antiracist views and beliefs" (ibid). Anti-racist for Kendi also means "learning about and identifying inequities and disparities that give, in particular, white people, or any racial group, material advantages over people of color" (ibid.). In summary, being antiracist means viewing racial groups as equals, but also pressing for policy changes that provide more racial equity and racial equality in a given society.

As I frequently touch upon in my invited talks around the United States and the world, Muhammad was much more than merely a non-racist. He was an anti-racist.

Muhammad's views on anti-racism come to life through his friendship with Bilal ibn Rabah, an Ethiopian slave who rose to a leading position in the early *ummah*. One story relates that Muhammad defended Bilal after Abu Dharr al-Ghifari, one of the Prophet's companions, after he despairingly referred to Bilal as "the son of a black woman." Concerned with the emphasis that he placed on skin color, Muhammad said to al-Ghifari, "you are a man who still has the traits of ignorance in him." Muhammad's reference to ignorance refers to the pre-Islamic period known as *jahiliyyah*, an Arabic term meaning the "state of ignorance." This period of history, before Muhammad's arrival, was marked by racism.

Bilal commanded so much respect among his peers that his fellow Muslims referred to him as "master." He eventually became the *muezzin*, or the community leader responsible for calling Muslims to the five daily prayers.[31] In choosing Bilal to serve in this honorable position, Muhammad made it clear that excluding racial minorities from positions of power, simply because they are racial minorities, is not condoned in Muslim societies.

Muhammad's fondness of Bilal is seen further in Bilal's marriage story. When an Arab family came to ask the Prophet for a suitable husband for their daughter, he suggested them to consider Bilal. The family, however, did not want to marry her to Bilal because he was black. The family did not say anything in response to Muhammad and decided to leave his presence. They later came to Muhammad two more times. The Prophet suggested Bilal on both occasions. In doing so, the Prophet taught that human beings should remember that a couple is made up of two people, not two races or cultures, and that the institution of marriage should not be predicated on ideas of racial superiority. This story reveals how Muhammad understood the struggle against racism as one that required structural and policy changes, not mere condemnations of something like racial slurs. After all, as Ibram X. Kendi told the National Public Radio (NPR), "[no] group in history has gained their freedom through appealing to the moral conscience of their oppressors [alone]."

The Farewell Sermon (see Appendix 2) of Muhammad, delivered in front of the *ummah* at Mount Arafat in 632, is another noteworthy manifestation of the Prophet's stance on anti-racism. He stated in the sermon: "An Arab has no superiority over a non-Arab, nor a non-Arab has any superiority over an Arab... a white person has no superiority over a black, nor does a black have any superiority over white except by piety and good action" (see Appendix 2).

Muhammad's speech preceded the famous words of Dr. Martin Luther King Jr., the African American civil rights activist and Christian reverend, who delivered his "I Have a Dream Speech" at the

Abraham Lincoln Memorial in Washington, DC in 1963. Dr. King said: "I have a dream that my four little children will one day live in a nation where they will not be judged by the color of their skin but by the content of their character." Both Muhammad and King placed emphasis on the importance of human beings' morals and actions rather than simply the color of their skin or perceived racial background.

The Prophet's views on racial equality and anti-racism are also seen through Malcolm X's life. Also known as El-Hajj Malik El-Shabazz, Malcolm X was an African American Muslim minister and human rights activist who was a well-known public figure during the Civil Rights Movement in the United States. Born Malcolm Little, he grew up in a home in which his father, Earl Little, was an outspoken Baptist minister and avid support of Black Nationalist leader Marcus Garvey.[32] As a young man, Malcolm started getting into trouble with various arrests and felony convictions. During his prison stint in Boston, he converted to the Nation of Islam (NOI), a black nationalist organization that uses the Islamic faith as a source for their social revolution and political philosophy.

As one of the NOI's most vocal leaders during the period of the Jim Crow laws, Malcolm X advocated for black pride, black self-sufficiency, black nationalism, and self-segregation of the black community. But his views on these matters changed when he performed *hajj*, the Islamic pilgrimage. While in Mecca he wrote a letter to his assistants in Harlem. The letter read:

> Never have I witnessed such sincere hospitality and overwhelming spirit of true brotherhood as is practiced by people of all colors and races here in this ancient Holy Land, the home of Abraham, Muhammad, and all the other Prophets of the Holy Scriptures. For the past week, I have been utterly speechless and spellbound by the graciousness I see displayed all around me by people of all colors… There were tens of thousands of pilgrims, from all over the world. They were of all colors, from blue-eyed blondes to black-skinned Africans. But we were all participating in the same ritual, displaying a spirit of unity and brotherhood that my experiences in America had let me to believe never could exist between the white and non-white [peo-

ple]... America needs to understand Islam, because this is the one religion that erases from its society the race problem. Throughout my travels in the Muslim world, I have met, talked to, and even eaten with people who in America would have been considered white – but the white attitude was removed from their minds by the religion of Islam. I have never before seen sincere and true brotherhood by all colors together, irrespective of their color.

Malcolm X continued by stating that his *hajj* experience forced him to rearrange his thought-patterns on the matter of racial equality, according to the Islamic tradition. After seeing the various races interacting in harmony under the guise of humanity, he could no longer keep a closed mind and reject the knowledge right in front of him.

These stories on racial equality and anti-racism provide much hope for the future. They remind us that human beings, as part of God's creation, are united in their common humanity, regardless of race or ethnicity. As is evident from Muhammad's actions, and the many Muslims who have followed in his footsteps, the Islamic faith has the power to fundamentally transform race relations here on Earth.

Chapter Four

Seeking Knowledge

T he Islamic faith, as noted in the Introduction, places great importance on the virtue of seeking knowledge. According to
scholar Mohammad Hossein Faryab, acquiring and possess-
ing knowledge, or *'ilm* in Arabic, is highly encouraged by the Holy
Qur'an and *Hadith*. God, for instance, introduces Himself using the
adjective "All-Knowing," or *'aleem*, 122 times in the holy text (Faryab
2012: 73). The very first verse of the Holy Qur'an revealed to Muhammad in 610 reads: "Read in and with the Name of your Lord,
Who has created. Created human from a clot clinging (to the wall
of the womb). Read, and your Lord is the All-Munificent, Who has
taught (human) by the pen. Taught human what he did not know"
(Qur'an 96:2-5). Similarly, the Holy Qur'an stresses that "God will
raise (in degree) those of you who truly believe (and act accordingly), and in degrees, those who have been granted the knowledge"
(Qur'an 58:11). Several *hadith* also highlight the importance of seeking knowledge:

> "Seeking knowledge is an obligation upon every Muslim" (Al-Tir-
> midhi).

> "The excellence of a scholar over another (ordinary) worshipper is
> like the excellence of the full moon over the rest of the heavenly bod-
> ies" (Abu Dawood).

> "Whoever treads a path in seeking knowledge, Allah will make easy
> for him the path to Paradise" (Al-Tirmidhi).

One of the more popular *hadiths*, "Seek knowledge, even if you have to go to China," is further evidence of Muhammad's emphasis on learning and education. While some critics raise the question of the authenticity of the *Hadith* at large, there can be no doubt as to the longstanding rich history of *'ilm* in the Islamic tradition.

Yet there are human beings around the world who appear to have forgotten the importance of knowledge in the Islamic tradition, and the contributions that Muslims have made to world civilization. Sam Harris, for example, a popular critic of the Islamic faith, referred to Malala Yousafzai, the Pakistani women's rights and education activist, as "the best thing to come out of the Muslim world in 1,000 years." Hidden in this comment is the idea that Malala's fellow Muslims are backward and that their Islamic faith is not conducive to change or progress achieved by means of knowledge and education.

The facts, however, show that Muslims have actually made revolutionary contributions to world civilization. Human beings who forget or willfully ignore these contributions can be said to suffer from "historical amnesia."[33]

Malala's quest for universal education follows the long and proud history of Muslim women working in the fields of education. A Muslim woman, Fatima Al-Fihri, started the world's first degree granting university, Al-Qarawiyyin in Fez, Morocco, in 859.[34] After inheriting a small fortune after the death of her father, Fatima invested in the founding of a mosque and institution for the enhancement of knowledge. Students from around the world were schooled at Al-Qarawiyyin in a number of religious and secular subjects including astronomy, grammar, the *Hadith*, languages, mathematics, medicine, and the Holy Qur'an. At the end of the program, teachers evaluated students and awarded degrees based on their performances. Numerous scholars are said to have studied at this intellectual center during the medieval period. One rumor is that Gerbert of Aurillac, better known as Pope Sylvester II – studied at al-Qarawiyyin, and it is he who is given the credit of introducing Arabic numerals to the rest of Europe.[35]

Muslims living during the Islamic Golden Age in al-Andalus (i.e. "Muslim Spain") were especially strong advocates of knowledge. Between the 8th and 15th centuries, al-Andalus was one of the world's centers of learning. Universities such as those in Cordoba, Granada, and Seville enrolled Jewish, Christian, and Muslim students who learned about a range of subjects largely from Muslim teachers. Women were also encouraged to study in al-Andalus.

One of the greatest contributions of Muslims to civilization started in al-Andalus during the 8th century when Muslim scholars inherited volumes of Greek philosophy texts. The knowledge in these texts, which had been lost to Europeans for centuries, was translated from Latin to Arabic by Muslim scholars, thus creating one of the greatest transmissions of wisdom in world history. Muslim scholars eventually brought the ideas of Socrates, Aristotle, and Plato to the European continent, where Greek philosophy was translated into various European languages. This process of knowledge transmission is the reason why scholars say that Muslims represent the main threshold behind the European Renaissance and later the Enlightenment, two periods of history that resurrected Greek philosophy and gave new life to a European continent that was bogged down by religious dogma and bloody religious conflicts.[36]

Under the Abbasid caliphate,[37] Muslims formed the vanguard of world civilization. During this period the Muslim world became "the unrivalled intellectual center for science, philosophy, medicine, and education" as the Abbasids championed the cause of knowledge by establishing Darul Hukama ("House of Wisdom") in their capital of Baghdad, in present-day Iraq (Wani and Maqbool 2012). The House of Wisdom held scholarly texts from Greece, Persia, and India. By the mid-9th century Baghdad became the intellectual center of the civilized world.

In addition to the library of the House of Wisdom, there were many other libraries in the capital, each of which contained thousands of books and manuscripts (ibid). Private individual libraries owned and operated by Muslims were also made available to leading scientists, philosophers, researchers, and writers (Naji 1968). Similar libraries were found in "Muslim Spain," as scholar of "Moorish Europe" Samuel Parsons Scott explains:

Nor must the libraries be omitted from this list of those factors of progress which so signally contributed to the public enlightenment and to the formation of national character. There was no [Spanish] city of importance without at least one of these treasure houses of literature. Their shelves were open to every applicant. Catalogues facilitated the examination of the collections and the classification of the various subjects. Many of the volumes were enriched with illuminations of wonderful beauty; the more precious were bound in the embossed leather and fragrant woods; some were inlaid with gold and silver. Here were to be found all the learning of the past and all the discoveries of the present age, the philosophy of Athens, the astronomy of Babylon, the science of Alexandria, the results of prolonged observation and experiment on the towers and in the laboratories of Cordoba and Seville (Scott 1904: 470).

By the 10th century, the Spanish city of Cordoba is said to have had at least 70 libraries, the largest of which had an impressive collection of 600,000 books, in addition to approximately 60,000 treaties, poems, polemics, and compilations that were published in an annual manner. Furthermore, the Cairo library is said to have housed 100,000 books, while the Tripoli library, which was destroyed by the Christians during the Crusades, is reported to have had three million books (Draper 1878: 138).

Al-Ghazali, the Sufi Muslim, is perhaps the most notable Muslim scholar who dedicated his life to engaging with Greek philosophical texts. In the 11th and 12th centuries, al-Ghazali helped to revolutionize early Islamic philosophy by developing Neoplatonism, which is understood to be the "mystical" or "religious" interpretation of philosophers like Socrates, Aristotle, and Plato. Muslim philosophers, at the time of al-Ghazali's writing, had read about the ideas coming out of Ancient Greece, but these ideas were generally perceived to be in conflict with traditional Islamic teachings. Al-Ghazali helped to synthesize the Islamic faith and Greek philosophy by adopting the techniques of Aristotelian logic, but he also diminished the influence of excessive rationalism in Greek philosophy.

The city of Cairo also served as an epicenter for scholars and students throughout the "Muslim world." Al-Azhar University, founded by the Fatimids in 970, was revived in the 13th century by the Mam-luk dynasty.[38] Famous scholars like Moses Maimonides, the Jewish philosopher who lectured on medicine and astronomy during the time of Saladin the Great in the 12th century, spent time learning in Cairo. In the 14th and 15th centuries Al-Azhar University and Cairo became hubs for Muslim scholars that fled Spain during the reign of the Castilian army, which destroyed Islamic centers of learning in Spanish cities like Cordoba, Granada, and Seville.[39] According to scholar Roger Boase, by the turn of the 16th century, Muslim re-ligious leaders handed over more than 5,000 priceless books with ornamental bindings, which were then consigned to flames. Only some books on medicine were spared.

Ibn Khaldun is another important Muslim scholar who lifted the European continent out of the Dark Ages. Recognized as one of the greatest historians and founders of the social sciences in the 14th and 15th centuries, Ibn Khaldun wrote *Muqaddimah*, one of the earliest secular philosophies in history.[40] Published in 1377, *Muqad-dimah* provided an early view of world history, but it also covered Islamic theology, the philosophy of history, and cultural history. Ibn Khaldun's book also helped pave the way for present day expecta-tions of presidents or prime ministers by creating a framework to evaluate "good rulers" by stating: "the sovereign exists for the good of the people... The necessity of a Ruler arises from the fact that human beings have to live together and unless there is someone to maintain order, society would break to pieces."

Development of medicine is another contribution made by Muslims to world civilization. In 872, in what is today Cairo, the Ahmad ibn Tulun hospital opened its doors. Like other hospitals that soon followed, Tulun was a secular institution open to men and women, adults and children, rich and poor, as well as Jews, Chris-tians, Muslims, and even atheists. Tulun also is said to be one of the first hospitals in history to provide care for human beings struggling with mental health challenges.

One hundred years after the Tulun founding, a surgeon named al-Zahrawi, often called the "father of surgery," wrote an illustrated encyclopedia that would ultimately be used as a guide for European surgeons for the next five hundred years. Al-Zahrawi's surgical instruments, including scalpels, bone saws, and forceps, are still used by present day surgeons. He is also believed to be the first surgeon in world history to perform a cesarean operation.

Another significant discovery came in the 13th century when Ibn Nafis, a medic, described the pulmonary circulation almost three hundred years before William Harvey, the English physician who is believed by many Westerners to have discovered it. The technique of inoculation, or the introduction of an antigenic substance or vaccine into the body to induce immunity to a disease, is said to have been designed by Muslims of the Ottoman Empire and brought to Western Europe by Lady Montagu, the wife of England's ambassador to the empire, in 1724.

Protecting and cleansing the body has always been a priority for Muslims. Perhaps, then, it is no surprise that Muslim scientists combined vegetable oils with sodium hydroxide and aromatics such as thyme oil to design a recipe for soap, which is still used today. Shampoo was also introduced on the seafront of Brighton, a city in southeastern England, in 1759 at Mahomed's Indian Vapour Baths.

There is also little doubt that the field of astronomy owes a great deal to the inventions of Muslims. As far back as the early 9th century, the Caliph al-Ma'mun founded astronomical observatories in Baghdad and Damascus. Five hundred years later, in 1420, Prince Ulugh Bey built a massive observatory in Samarkand,[41] which was then followed in 1577 by another observatory built by Sultan Murad III in Constantinople, the former capitol of the Ottoman Empire and the present-day city of Istanbul, Turkey. The Ottomans had particularly strong astronomical institutions including the post of chief-astronomer and time-keeping houses. Taqi al-Din, a 16th-century Ottoman astronomer, created astronomical tables and observational instruments that helped measure the coordinates of stars and the distances between them.

Muslims also made significant contributions in the field of chemistry by inventing many of the basic processes and apparatuses used by present-day chemists. Working in the 8th and 9th centuries in al-Andalus, Jabir ibn Hayyan, widely considered to be the founder of modern chemistry, transformed alchemy into chemistry through distillation, the process of separating liquids through differences in their boiling points. In addition to developing the processes of crystallization, evaporation, and filtration, he also discovered sulphuric and nitric acid. The historian Erick John Holmyard stated that ibn Hayyan's work is as important, if not more so, than that of Robert Boyle and Antoine Lavoisier, two European chemists who are frequently attributed with creating "modern chemistry."

Finally, today's globalized world would not be able to move so quickly if it were not for the genius of Ibn Firnas, a Muslim engineer of al-Andalus, who in the 9th century constructed a flying machine, thus becoming the world's first aviator. In 852 he is said to have jumped from the minaret of the Grand Mosque in Cordoba by using a loose cloak stiffened with wooden struts. Although he hoped to glide like an eagle, Ibn Firnas did not, but he is nevertheless credited for creating the first parachute.

The inventions and scientists highlighted above only scratch the surface of the contributions made by Muslims towards the development of Western civilization and world civilization. Ahmed Essa captures the role that Muslims played throughout history in his book *Studies in Islamic Civilization: The Muslim Contribution to the Renaissance*:

> ... of one thing there is no doubt whatsoever. No scholar, whatever his or her background and learning, will ever be able to alter or delete the achievements of Islamic civilization and its contribution to, and its place in, world history. All other civilizations, especially that of the West, which followed the Islamic example benefited from these achievements... the West borrowed overwhelmingly from Islam and the Muslim world and benefited immensely from those borrowings (Essa, 2010: 256).

"The Other al-Andalus"[42]

While al-Andalus is represented as the pinnacle of religious pluralism, there is another piece of history – too often ignored and still only adequately assessed – coming out of Sicily, an island belonging to the present-day country of Italy. The unique culture that developed in Sicilian society is hardly mentioned in the annals of European, Christian, or Islamic history. Yet the interreligious and cross-cultural exchanges in the fields of science and religion produced a hybrid culture that borrowed from Arab, Byzantine, Christian, Islamic, and Norman traditions.

Sicily, for a period of time during the Middle Ages, represented the crossroads between East and West as well as the Islamic faith and Christian faith. In short, "the Other al-Andalus" (Sicily) represented the kind of society, anchored in cross-cultural interactions and the energetic engagement with religious diversity, that Muhammad had envisioned in the 7th century.

Muslims and the Islamic faith are rarely associated with Italian or European history, but Islamic contact with Sicily began approximately twenty years after the death of Muhammad during the caliphate of 'Uthman. The Syrian governor at the time, Mu'awiya, ordered a naval expedition to Sicily as an extension of the battles that were taking place in the east between the Muslim army and the Byzantine army. For about two hundred years after the initial contact, Muslims tried to control the island, then a Byzantine province, but to no avail. It was not until 827 that Muslims finally obtained a foothold when they captured Mazara Del Vallp, a city on the southwestern side of the island. The successful military expedition was launched from Ifriqiya, a North African province of the Islamic Empire and the present-day country of Tunisia.

Unlike al-Andalus, which fell to the Muslim army like a ripe piece of fruit, the Islamic takeover of Sicily happened over the span of seventy-five years. Once the Muslims secured the island, their leadership divided the land into three administrative districts, the names of which survive to this day. The first district, Mazara del Vallo, comprises the western coast. The city of Palermo was named the capital of the region. The central region of Sicily – including the city of Syracuse – was given the name Val Di Noto, while the remaining region (and the last to be conquered) was called Val Demone. The cities of Catania and Messina are located in Val Demone. The word *val* is derived from the Arabic word meaning "province."

Three Muslim-led dynasties ruled Sicily until 1017. The first group to rule were the Aghlabids, an Ifriqiyan Sunni family that had broken away from the Abbasid caliphate that was based in Baghdad, in present-day Iraq. Following the Aghlabids were the Fatimids, a Shi'ite group that drove out their predecessors in 909 and founded their Sicilian base of Mahdia in 916. The Fatimids eventually conquered Egypt in 969 and transferred the seat of the caliphate from Baghdad to the newly founded city of Cairo in 973. The Fatimid *emir*, or governor, later ruled Ifriqiya and Sicily.

Under these Muslim-led dynasties, the Sicilian population grew rapidly and dozens of towns and cities were founded and repopulated, including Castrogiovanni, Mazara, Messina, Sciacca, and Syracuse. The most important Sicilian city, Palermo, was described in the following manner by Ibn Jubair, a Muslim geographer, traveler, and poet from al-Andalus:

> [Palermo] is endowed with two gifts, splendor and wealth. It contains all the real and imagined beauty that anyone could wish. Splendor and grace adorn the piazzas and the countryside; the streets and highways are wide, and the eye is dazzled by the beauty of its situation. It is a city full of marvels, with buildings similar to those of Cordoba, built of limestone. A permanent stream of water from four springs runs through the city. There are so many mosques that they are impossible to count. Most of them also serve as schools. The eye is dazzled by all this splendor.

Much of the growth and expansion of Palermo was due to agricultural and technological innovations. Muslims introduced new crops, including cotton, hemp, date palms, sugar cane, mulberries, and citrus fruits. The cultivation of these crops was made possible by new irrigation techniques. These agricultural innovations spurned other industries including textiles, sugar manufacture, rope-making as well as silk and paper.

The Normans are an ethno-religious group that settled in northern France in the 10th century, particularly in the region of Normandy, from which the group gets its name. The Normans were descendants of the Vikings,[43] or Norsemen, who conquered and colonized a significant portion of the European continent including parts of

England, Ireland, Italy, Scotland, and Wales. The first Normans arrived in Italy about the year 1000 while returning to Western Europe from a pilgrimage to Jerusalem. The Norman arrival started with Prince Guaimar III of Salerno, who requested help in defending the town against Muslims. After defending Salerno, a small contingent of Normans remained in Italy. In 1016, the Norman Christians went for pilgrimage to the shrine of Saint Michael on Monte Gargano in Apulia, where they met Melus, also referred to in historical accounts as Ishmael, a leader of an anti-Byzantine rebellion in Bari. Melus asked the Normans to help him as he tried to free his town of Byzantine rule. Gradually, the Norman conquest took shape.

In 1061, a modest military force under the leadership of Robert Guiscard and Roger of Hauteville were paid by a Sicilian *emir*, Ibn al-Thumma, to assist Muslims in the civil war. At that time the island, which had a sizeable and rebellious Christian population, was split between three Muslim governors. The Normans eventually consolidated their power. In 1071 they captured the city of Palermo, and by 1091 the city of Noto and the island of Malta – the last Arab stronghold – were taken by the Norman Christians.

Roger II, the most notable Norman ruler of Sicily, was a descendant of Christian knights who previous Popes had recruited to fight Muslims around the Mediterranean region. Ruling as King of Sicily from 1130 to 1154, Roger II is considered by historians to be one of the most successful rulers in European history. He is said to have been a "product of the Mediterranean" in the sense that he was born and bred in a cosmopolitan, multilingual world of Greek and Muslim tutors and secretaries that organically influenced his hybrid identity. The language of his court was French, but all royal edicts were written in the language of the people they were addressed to: Latin, Greek, Arabic and Hebrew. Roger II is said to have spoken Arabic perfectly. In short, King Roger II's vision was "multicultural" long before multiculturalism became a fad in the "Western world."

The dissemination of knowledge and learning were key components of Roger II's Sicilian society. Astronomy, medicine, philosophy, and mathematics were some of the subjects discussed in Roger's palace. Books were translated into various languages and became the standard textbooks in 12th century universities that were popping up around Europe.

The emphasis placed on knowledge and education led to the founding of the University of Salerno in the 13th century. Salerno became one of the most foremost medical schools in the world. It was there that Ibn Sina, popularly referred to in the "Western world" by the Latin name Avicenna, wrote his famous work *Al-Qanun Fi al-Tibb*, or "The Canon of Medicine." Published in Latin towards the end of the twelfth century, *Al-Qanun* served as an important piece of scholarship that informed the educational development of medical students across the European continent for hundreds of years. Roger II also requested the help of Muslim troops and Arab siege engines during his military campaigns in southern Italy. Once his troops had conquered new land, he mobilized Arab architects to help Normans build monuments in a Norman-Arab-Byzantine style.

Artist techniques from the Islamic tradition were successfully incorporated to form the foundation of Arab-Norman art. The Church of Saint John of the Hermits is one of the greatest examples of the fusion of Arab and Norman architecture. Built by Roger II between 1143 and 1148 AD in Palermo, the Church of Saint John is famous for its red domes that clearly show the Arab artistic influence present in 12th century Sicilian society. In his "Diary of an Idle Woman in Sicily," Frances Elliot described the Church as "totally oriental... it would fit well in Baghdad or Damascus." Giuseppe Bellafior, former Dean of Architectural History at the University of Palermo, also echoes such observations:

> ... the purely Norman element in Arabo-Norman architecture is less than the name might suggest. The Norman rulers had the tact and the foresight to accept, and even like, what they found. Yet they retained the tenuous links which they had with the land of their origin. The strength and efficiency of the Norman administration derived from its policy of deliberate flexibility toward the existing Muslim order on the island. Thus, the culture in general, and artistic tradition in particular, owed little to the Norman's own land of origin.

King Roger was keen on using a range of cultural legacies in building a new Sicilian society. Muslim soldiers, poets, and scientists played important roles in his court and palace. Agricultural and industrial techniques developed by Arab Muslims over the previous two-hundred years also were used to further develop Sicilian art, economy, and culture.

The most famous book of his reign – *The Book of Roger* (also known as *Kitab Rudjdjar*) – was written in Arabic by Muhammad al-Idrisi, an Arab Muslim geographer. Al-Idrisi was based at the court of Roger, where he was charged with writing a book on geography and climate zones. *The Book of Roger* was monumental considering that al-Idrisi depicted the Earth as a sphere and hinted at the concept of gravity. In a testament to the book, historian S.P. Scott commented: "For three centuries geographers copied [al-Idrisi's] maps without alteration." Roger II, unfortunately, never lived to see its publication. Al-Idrisi's work appeared several weeks after the great ruler of Sicily passed away in 1154.

Roger II's greatest legacy was a series of laws called "Assizes of Ariano," which passed in 1140 and were derived from Norman, French, Muslim, and Byzantine legal theories. These laws were advanced in the context of the 12th century, because all Sicilians were equal under the law, regardless of whether they were of Latin, Greek, Jewish, Muslim, Norman, Lombard, or Arab descent. Roger, in-turn, fostered pluralism towards non-Christians, a tradition carried over from Muhammad's rule in Medina. This pluralism led to dialogue and a climate of intellectual freedom that was the envy of the world, as John Julius Norwich, a historian on Norman Sicily, remarked:

> Norman Sicily stood forth in Europe – and indeed in the whole bigoted medieval world – as an example of tolerance and enlightenment, a lesson in the respect that every man should feel for those whose blood and beliefs happen to differ from his own.

The acceptance that Norman Christians showed towards people of other faith traditions was unusual for the 12th century. Sicilian Muslims were granted rights to live according to the *sharia*, particularly the Maliki school. Al-Mazari, one particular *qadi* (or magistrate), reciprocated by ruling that Muslim jurists appointed by Christians had legal force and should be obeyed unconditionally. Muslims in Christian-ruled Sicily retained both social status and legal authority within their own communities. While the Norman Christians did deploy a slightly higher tax on Muslims than Christians, Muslims were nevertheless granted property rights and legal protection under the law. By enforcing a tax to help protect Muslims, the Christians of 12th century Sicily adopted a similar fiscal and legal structure as the Islamic *jizya* and *dhimmi*.

One of the most inspiring stories coming out of Norman Sicily occurred under the rule of William II, Roger II's grandson. Ibn Jubair, the Muslim geographer, traveler, and poet from al-Andalus, visited the Sicilian coast after embarking on a pilgrimage to Mecca in 1184.[44] Shipwrecked in the Straits of Messina off the Sicilian coast, Jubair and other Muslims were in danger of losing their lives to the wild sea. Local inhabitants of Messina heard their call of distress and immediately launched their boats to save them, however, as businessmen, they hoped to profit from the shipwreck by charging large fees to rescue the Muslim pilgrims. Faced with paying high fees, the Muslims could not afford the rescue effort and were ultimately faced with the possibility of dying at sea. At this moment, Ibn Jubair reports, a man rode down to the shore on horseback and delivered an order to the Messinians – the Muslim pilgrims were to be saved and taken safely to land. Astonished by the turn of events, Ibn Jubair went to thank the man who rode on horseback and discovered that he was King William II. The Norman Christian king welcomed Ibn Jubair and his fellow Muslims and promised them protection in Sicily.

Upon traveling the streets, Ibn Jubair observed that many Christians spoke Arabic and that William II's top government officials were mostly Muslims. "The attitude of [William II] is really extraordinary," Ibn Jubair commented, "His attitude towards the Muslims is perfect; he gives them employment, he chooses his officers among them, and all, or almost all... can remain faithful to the faith of Islam." Ibn Jubair continues: "[William II] has full confidence in the Muslims and relies on them to handle his affairs, including the most important ones, to the point that the Great Intendant for cooking is a Muslim." Not only did William II produce coins in Arabic with Hegira dates, but the registers of the Royal Court were also written in Arabic.

Like rulers before him, Frederick II, the Holy Roman Emperor and grandson to Roger II, based his administration in Sicily. By birth, he was of half-German, half-Norman ancestry. Brought up in his mother's birthplace of Sicily, Frederick II was bred in a half-Arab, half-Greek culture. As such, he is said to have united elements of the Islamic and Christian traditions. Not only did he speak Arabic and Greek, but Frederick also spoke Latin, German, French, and Sicilian. Herbert George Wells,[45] the prolific English author, historian, and sociologist, wrote that, "Frederick II came to an Islamic point of view of Christianity and to a Christian one of Islam." Frederick also is described by a contemporary chronicle as *stupor mondi*, the Latin phrase for "the wonder of the world," and by Frederick Nietzsche as "the first European."

Frederick is known for the Constitutions of Melfi, written in 1231, and also referred to as *Liber Augustalis*. The Melfi constitution is a collection of laws that remained the standard in Sicily until 1819. Building on his grandfather's "Assizes of Ariano," the Constitutions of Melfi declared "equality before the law" of all citizens of the Kingdom of Sicily. Other highlights of this legal code included setting up a loyal Muslim community and army in Lucera and declaring the equality before the law for Jews in the Sicilian kingdom.

Frederick II is further recognized for his cordial relations with Muslims. He is said to have been initiated into Sufi mysticism of the Islamic faith. In 1228, Frederick decided to embark on a crusade to Palestine, but this was not your typical, violent crusade as depicted in Hollywood movies. His journey is the only historical Crusade without violence. In Cairo, Frederick II met with the Egyptian Sultan Malik al-Kamil, who shared Frederick's interest of poetry, philosophy, and chess. As a token of his respect for the Islamic tradition, Frederick II presented the Sultan with one of his beloved falcons and received an elephant in return. Resulting from the meeting between these leaders was an armistice and treaty signed on 18 February 1229. Frederick II was given control of holy sites in Jerusalem, Bethlehem, and Nazareth. The treaty also stipulated that the Dome of the Rock and al-Aqsa mosque were to remain under Muslim control. This was a bloodless victory for both Christians and Muslims. This simple diplomatic exchange accomplished more than violence had ever done in terms of Christian and Muslim relations, hence why historian Humbert Fink wrote the following about Frederick's legacy: "[He] was the only Western sovereign and monarch who did not approach the East and the Arabs with the sword but with the art of persuasion and empathy attempted what up to now always had cost flows of blood."

Just as it was during centuries ago, Sicily continues to show elements of a hybrid culture formed through the transmission of knowledge. Even to this day one can see living traces of the past in Sicily. Place names such as Alcantra (from the Arabic word *qantara*, or bridge) and Gibellina (from the Arabic word, *jabal*, or mountain) are two such examples. Many street names are still recognizably Arabic, and in some cases, not only the original name, but the function of the street, has been preserved. The district of Lattarini in Palermo has harbored perfumers and grocers since the 9th century. The Muslims called this district *suq al-ʿattarin*, the market of the perfumers.

The history of Sicily punches far above its weight; it is one of the world's main centers of Christian and Muslim encounters. Pluralism flourished on this island during the Islamic "Golden Age" and during some of Europe's darkest days. Sicily can no doubt remind us that East and West – as well as the Islamic and Christian faiths – are not mutually exclusive entities. Quite the opposite – they have fused together to create some of the greatest civilizations the Earth has ever seen.

Rumi and Emerson: A bridge between civilizations[46]

The lives of Jalalud'din Rumi, the 13th century Sufi Muslim poet and philosopher from present-day Afghanistan, and Ralph Waldo Emerson, the 19th century Christian transcendentalist from Boston, Massachusetts, are filled with lessons that can enrich every single human soul. Rumi's and Emerson's views on a range of topics, including pluralism, love, and knowledge, can serve as a bridge for the perceived chasm between "Western civilization" and the "Muslim world."

Rumi has been known throughout history as one of the foremost scholars of the Islamic tradition, particularly its mystical and existential branches. Rumi dedicated his life to spreading the Holy Qur'an's peaceful message and sharing Muhammad's egalitarian teachings with humanity. One of Rumi's well-known couplets is: "I am the slave of the Holy Qur'an as long as I shall live. I am the soil under the feet of Prophet Muhammad."[47] And, according to John Baldock, if we wish to understand the inner meaning of the life of the Prophet and the principal tenets of Islam, we have no better teacher than Rumi (Baldock 2006: 54).

As a young man, Rumi was trained to become a theologian, but he later focused more on writing poetry steeped in Islamic mysticism after meeting his mentor, Shams Tabrizi, in 1244. Rumi conveyed his mystical views primarily through poems, many of which speak to the infinite love he had for humanity. In the essay "He Was in No Other Place," Rumi shared his views on God and humanity at large:

> Cross and Christians, end to end, I examined.
> He was not on the Cross.
> I went to the Hindu temple, to the ancient pagoda.
> In none of them was there any sign.
> To the uplands of Herat I went,
> and to Kandahar I looked.
> He was not on the heights or in the lowlands.
> Resolutely, I went to the summit of the [fabulous] mountain of Kaf.
> There only was the dwelling of the [legendary] Anqa bird.
> I went to the Ka'ba of Mecca.
> He was not there.
> I asked about him from Avicenna, the philosopher.
> He was beyond the range of Avicenna...
> I looked into my heart.
> In that place, his place, I saw him.
> He was in no other place.

This verse, as described by Wahab Owolawi, captures Rumi's spirit and views on the "religion of love." In the religion of love, there is nothing like "believers" or "non-believers." The religion of love, as Owolawi continues, implies:

> ... an all-embracing concept regardless of one's faith, belief, or philos-
> ophy. Religion of love neither labels, discriminates, nor compartmen-

talizes. Permit me to also add that there's only one authentic religion in life, the religion of love and service. Anything to the contrary is an aberration. When next someone asks you what religion you believe in, simply answer LOVE. While religion of love is of the sublime, religion of separation or segmentation is of the mundane (Owolawi 2017 n.p.).

Rumi's love of humanity embraced the idea that all religions were more or less equal because they all captured elements of the divine truth, which he explains below:

I am neither Christian, nor Jewish, nor Muslim
I am not of the East, nor of the West...
I have put duality away, I have seen the two worlds as one;
One I seek,
One I know,
One I see,
One I call.

In this passage Rumi eliminates any kind of bias based upon religion or race. He proposes a brotherhood that unites all human beings under one faith – what we may refer to as the metaphysical meaning of *tawhid* (oneness), which indicates the transcendence of the essence of religion over all its outward forms, including even that of the Islamic faith (Shah-Kazemi 2012). Rumi's views reflect what we today refer to, in the traditional sense, as pluralism, or the belief that no single religious tradition has a monopoly on the truth. We may think Rumi was emphasizing that there are many ways through which people come into contact with the Creator, and that the Islamic faith is not the only faith that offers a path to heaven.

Rumi's funeral in Konya, Turkey in 1273 is another example of the strength of our common humanity. People from all walks of life came to pay their respect to the legendary Sufi poet. According to tradition a weeping Muslim man approached a Christian man at the funeral and asked him, "Why are you crying at the funeral of a Muslim poet?" The Christian responded back: "We esteemed him as the Moses, the David, the Jesus of the age. We are all his followers and his disciples." Rumi was popular among his peers because he saw them as human beings first rather than simply Jews, Christians, or Muslims.

Ralph Waldo Emerson, like Rumi, devoted his young adulthood to studying the theological underpinnings of the various faith traditions of the world. As a young adult he studied to be a Unitarian Minister at the Harvard University Divinity School, where he was considered by many of his peers as too "radical" because of his post-Christian philosophical beliefs. In his posthumously published journals, Emerson stated that "[the] heart of Christianity is at the heart of all philosophy," but he also credited the stoics, Chinese, Muslims, and Hindus for laboring to awaken human souls to the Creator. Further, in his essay "Essential Principles of Religion," he shows an appreciation for the noble saints among "the Buddhist, the [Muslim], the highest stoic of Athens, the purest and wisest Christian…" Emerson added that if these saints "could meet somewhere and converse, they would all find themselves of one religion," which reminds us again of Emerson's belief in the oneness of humanity.

Emerson's essays, "Love" and "Heroism," carry epigraphs linking his philosophy to the Islamic faith. "Love" begins with Emerson selecting the "Koran" as a suitable example of pure love: "I was as a gem concealed; Me my burning ray revealed."[48] "Heroism" begins with an epigraph from Muhammad: "O people! Do not wish to face the enemy and ask Allah to save you (from calamities); but if you should face the enemy, then be patient and let it be known to you that Paradise is under the shadow of swords." Emerson did not, however, perceive Muhammad as a violent person, as many present-day critiques of him do. Instead, Emerson portrayed the Prophet as a man of self-control, as he noted in "Man the Reformer": "Every great and commanding moment in the annals of the world is the triumph of some enthusiasm. The victories of the Arabs after [Muhammad], who in a few years, from a small and mean beginning, established a larger empire than that of Rome, is an example." Here Emerson suggests that the ascendancy of the Islamic faith was due to its universalist appeal instead of violence and war. Emerson, as Russell B. Goodman noted on the Oxford University Press's blog, regarded the Holy Qur'an as a sacred text and work of poetry that influenced world history because of Muhammad's enthusiasm for transforming humanity.[49]

Emerson also translated approximately 700 lines of Persian poetry, most of which were written by Hafiz, the 14th century Sufi Persian poet who expressed in his poems love for the divine and oneness of humanity. Emerson also described Hafiz as "a name of anecdote and courage… [a sally] of freedom." Hafiz appears again in Emerson's essay, "History," in which he is placed among the major writers and thinkers of the world, alongside Homer, the legendary Greek author of the *Odyssey*, and Geoffrey Chaucer, the fourteenth century English poet and author of *The Canterbury Tales*. Moreover, in his journal, Emerson characterized Hafiz as a person with "perfect intellectual emancipation" and someone who "fears nothing." Emerson added, "He sees too far… such is the only man I wish to see and to be."

Emerson also had a particular interest in Hindu spirituality throughout his life. In fact, it is said that much of his philosophy on "oneness," known by the Arabic term *tawhid* in the Islamic tradition, is borrowed from Hindu scripture. For Emerson, the concept of oneness is found in all nations in which "there are minds [that] incline to dwell in the conception of the fundamental unity." This tendency, he stated in his journal, "finds its highest expression in the religious writings of the East, and chiefly in the Indian scriptures, in the Vedas, the *Bhagavad Gita*, and the *Vishnu Purana*…" Emerson singled out the *Bhagavad Gita*, which to him was "an empire of thought" and a book that had "the voice of an old intelligence."

Looking closer at Rumi's writing, we also find the theme of oneness or *tawhid*. He wrote in his poem, "One Song:"

> What is praised is one,
> So that praise is one too,
> Many jugs being poured into a huge basin.
> All religions, all this singing, one song.

In another poem, "All Religions Are But One," he offered the following words:

> Since the object of praise is one,
> From this point of view,
> all religions are but one religion.

Know that all praise belongs to the Light of God
and is only lent to created forms and beings.
Should people praise anyone but the One
who alone deserves to be praised?
But they go astray in useless fantasy.
The Light of God in relation to phenomena
is like light shining upon a wall –
the wall is but a focus for these splendors.

Emerson's theory of oneness is again clearly visible in his essay, "Over-soul," in which he argued that all mankind should be united like "the water of the globe, [being] all one, and, truly seen, its tide is one." Emerson's transcendental philosophy of oneness was additionally influenced by his experience in the natural wonders of Massachusetts, which helped him connect to a deeper mystical union between himself and the universe.

The essay "Over-soul" also shared Emerson's desire for all people in the world to peacefully unite and denounce war, which he called "an unnecessary foolishness, because just beyond the arguing there is a long table of companionship set and waiting for us to sit down." A striking similarity to Emerson's "Over-soul" is found in Rumi's poem "A Great Wagon," which reads:

Out beyond ideas of wronging and right doing,
there is a field. I'll meet you there.
When the soul lies down in that grass,
The world is too full to talk about.
Ideas, language, even the phrase *each other*
doesn't make any sense.

Emerson used an image of a table to represent the common ground of humanity in which peoples of all walks of life can meet. Rumi, on the other hand, used the image of a field. Both poets encouraged human beings to find common ground to foster connectivity and build friendships among the people of the world. Instead of focusing on differences, Emerson and Rumi stress the importance of compassion and communication, both of which can lead to respect and mutual trust.

The power of love also was foremost on Rumi's and Emerson's minds. James Cowan, an expert on Rumi's poetry, said that he was "[p]ossessed by such an overwhelming vision of love, [that] he was unable to confine himself to any one spiritual discipline for his inspiration." One of Rumi's poems, "Love is the Master," supports Cowan's assertion:

> Love is the One who masters all things;
> I am mastered totally by Love.
> By my passion of love for Love…

Another poem, "I am a child of love," reveals Rumi's understanding of the relationship between religion, love, and humanity:

> I profess the religion of love,
> Love is my religion and my faith.
> My mother is love
> My father is love
> My prophet is love
> My God is love
> I am a child of love
> I have come only to speak of love.

Rumi extended his love to people from all walks of life, regardless of ethnicity, cultural orientation, religious beliefs, or race. Inscribed on his shrine in Konya is the following verse:

> Come, come, whoever you are
> Wanderer, worshiper, lover of leaving.
> It doesn't matter.
> Ours is not a caravan of despair.
> Come, even if you have broken your vows a thousand times.
> Come, yet again, come, come.

Furthermore, for Rumi, God is the source of all love that permeates the universe. Love, for him, is:

... an infinite ocean whose skies are a bubble of foam.
Know that it is the waves of Love which makes the wheel of the
Heavens turn; without Love the world would be inanimate.
How is an inorganic thing transformed into a plant?
How are the plants sacrificed to become gifted with spirit?
How is the spirit sacrificed for the Breath, of which only a
Whiff was enough to impregnate Mary?
Each atom is intoxicated with this Perfection and hastens
Toward it... Their haste says implicitly: "Glory be to God."

Like Rumi, Emerson was inspired by the power of love, as seen
in his poem, "Give All to Love":

Give all to love;
Obey thy heart;
Friends, kindred, days,
Estate, good fame,
Plans, credit and the muse;
Nothing refuse.

Later in "Give All to Love," Emerson stated the following: "He
who is in love is wise and is becoming wiser."

Disdain for materialism and worldly pleasures is another common theme across the writings of Rumi and Emerson. In his poem
"Heart," Rumi criticized those who know "the value of every article of
merchandise," adding that, "if you don't know the value of your own
soul, it's all foolishness." Rumi believed that a person that is preoccu-
pied by possessions is a person that is enslaved by social status.

Emerson, too, spoke out against materialism. During an address
to the Phi Beta Kappa Society in Cambridge, Massachusetts in 1867,
he stated that "the spiritual is stronger than any material force" and
that "thoughts rule the world." In another lecture titled "Religion"
years earlier in 1836, Emerson portrayed Confucius, the Chinese
philosopher, as part of a class of heroes who pursued virtue instead
of "worldly riches."

Both Rumi's and Emerson's embrace of humanity is a useful example in a world today that is fractured, in many cases, along reli-

gious and racial lines. Their writings remind us of the confluence and dialogue of civilizations instead of the clash of civilizations, which Prophet Muhammad stood for long before Rumi and Emerson were alive. As Rumi said in his poem, "Look at Love:"

> Why are you so busy
> with this or that or good or bad
> pay attention to how things blend

If Rumi and Emerson were alive today, neither would take issue with praying in a house of worship outside of their immediate religious preferences. They encouraged human beings to search for their own personal connection with God through existential and wondrous ways. Their love for everyone and everything, regardless of who or what they were, reminds us that Christians and Muslims are not as different than many people seem to think and imagine.

CHAPTER FIVE

WOMEN'S RIGHTS

The rights of Muslim women in accordance with the *sharia* is a topic of much speculation. Media outlets around the world tend to depict Muslim women as helpless victims in the face of patriarchy and male dominance. Stories surrounding tragic events like honor killings, genital mutilation, and abuse of Muslim women only exacerbate the stereotype that the Islamic faith inherently looks down upon and mistreats women. On the contrary to these popular depictions, Muslim women are using their agency to distinguish themselves as free and independent members of our respective communities. In doing so they are following the teachings and legacy of Muhammad himself.

In a time when women had few, if any, rights in Arabia, Muhammad helped to liberate women with divinely sanctioned social, property, and marital rights. The Holy Qur'an, a book that shares the Word of God as presented to Muhammad, states that men and women were equal because they were created of a single soul:

> O humankind! In due reverence for your Lord, keep from disobedience to Him Who created you from a single human self, and from it created its mate, and from the pair of them, scattered abroad multitude of men and women. In due reverence for God, keep from disobedience to Him in Whose name you make demands of one another, and (duly observe) the rights of the wombs (i.e. of kinship), thus observing piety in your relations with God and with human beings). God is ever watchful over you (Qur'an 4:1).

Indeed, as scholar Karen Armstrong notes, the Holy Qur'an "gave women rights of inheritance and divorce centuries before Western women were accorded such status" (Armstrong 2000: 16).

Muhammad's views on the position of women in society were of course guided by God through revelation, but he also made sincere efforts to listen to women in the hope of alleviating some of their concerns as members of the early *ummah*. The women in Muhammad's midst once asked him questions about the Holy Qur'an that resulted in him receiving revelations from God. Arabic language has grammatical gender, and the male plural pronouns are inclusive of women unless it is specifically mentioned. The Holy Qur'an is in Arabic, so many of those male pronouns are about women, too. However, in at least a few narrations a Muslim woman (different names are mentioned in different narrations) approached Muhammad to alert him to their disappointment that the Holy Qur'an had too many references to male pronouns. The women were concerned that the pronouns meant only men could be "believers." They were either not aware of the grammatical rule, or they wanted to have assurance in their heart that the Qur'an was not only for men. Soon after this encounter, Muhammad received a revelation that placed women on equal footing with men. The Holy Qur'an notes:

> Surely all men and women who submit to God (whose submission is attested by their words and deeds), and all truly believing men and truly believing women, and all devoutly obedient men and devoutly obedient women, and all men and women honest and truthful in their speech (and true to their words in their actions), and all men and women who persevere (in obedience to God through all adversity), and all men and women humble (in mind and heart before God), and all men and women who give in alms (and in God's cause), and all men and women who fast (as an obligatory or commended act of devotion), and all men and women who guard their chastity (and avoid exposing their private parts), and all men and women who remember and mention God much for them (all), God has prepared forgiveness (to bring unforeseen blessings) and a tremendous reward (Qur'an 33:35).

The Prophet also requested that men treat their daughters and wives with the utmost dignity and respect, as he related in a *hadith*: "Do treat your women well and be kind to them." To hammer home his teaching, Muhammad ended female infanticide, a common practice in pre-Islamic Arab society, and provided women the right to both own and purchase land. These facts are why Pierre Crabitès,[50] a U.S. judge who was born in the French Quarter of New Orleans in 1873, said that "Mohammad was probably the greatest champion of women's rights the world has ever seen." Crabitès added: "Muhammad's outstanding contribution to the cause of women, resides in the property rights that he conferred upon the wives of his people… The Moslem spouse in so far as her property is concerned, is as free as a bird."

Muslim women in the formative years of the *ummah* were involved in some of the most important tasks in the development of society as well as the "Islamic state." Take, for example, the wives and daughters of Muhammad, who served in many roles including as businesswomen, warriors, consultants, and scholars. The first person in Islamic history to embrace the Islamic faith, for instance, is Khadijah, the Prophet's first wife, who managed a lucrative and extensive caravan trading business across the Hijaz and Arabian peninsula.

Any human being who wants to learn about Muhammad must study the relationship that he had with Khadijah, who also happened to be his boss. Imagine that. Muhammad actually worked for her successful trading caravan as a business representative. Khadijah even made the marriage proposal to Muhammad, a practice unheard of in the 7th century and even in the present-day.

Khadijah was an essential partner in Muhammad's evolution as a Prophet of God. After receiving his first revelation from the Angel Gabriel at Mount Hira in 610, Muhammad went home in a panic to be comforted by Khadijah. He was scared that he was losing his mind after interacting with Gabriel. Khadijah protected the Prophet during that difficult experience and ensured him that he was indeed chosen by God to lead the Arabs out of *jahiliyyah*. Khadijah became the first person to recognize Muhammad's prophecy. Her belief played a crucial role in the establishment of the Islamic faith.

Khadijah is certainly not the only woman in Islamic history to break ground in terms of a woman's place in society. While she supported him in the beginning of his prophethood in Mecca, Aisha bint Abu Bakr, another one of Muhammad's wives, wed and supported Muhammad after his migration to Medina. Aisha transmitted more than 2,000 *hadiths*. These narrations of the Prophet provide invaluable insight into his everyday practices and behavior. She went on to educate Muslims in the early years of the *ummah* on the Holy Qur'an and the example of Muhammad himself. Befitting the title of "the Mother of the Believers," Aisha braved the front lines in several battles including the Battles of Camel,[51] Uhud, Al-Khandaq, Banu Qurayza, Banu Mustaliq, Hudaybiya, and Mecca. This was an extraordinary feat considering that she was still very young during these major battles.

Aisha grew into womanhood during the last decade of Muhammad's life, in which the Prophet established her authority by telling Muslims to consult her in his absence. She was known during the time as a sharp and intelligent person. Aisha knew the Holy Qur'an and *Sunnah* by heart. Whenever she emerged victorious in an intellectual conversation, the Prophet would smile and say, "She is the daughter of Abu Bakr!"

Although she remained quiet during her father's and Umar's reigns, as the first and the second caliphs respectively, Aisha emerged as a vocal critic of Uthman's and Ali's leadership. Following her short stint in the political and public realms, Aisha turned to more scholarly activities by narrating thousands of *hadiths*, which significantly spread her influence among the early *ummah*.

In summary, Aisha was a "stateswoman, scholar, mufti, and judge, [who] combined spirituality, activism and knowledge."[52] As such, she remains a role model for many Muslim women in the 21st century and beyond.

Unveiling the veil

Veiling, the practice of covering one's body with a scarf or similar form of clothing, was a customary practice among the Arab people and countless other cultures before the coming of the Islamic faith in the 7th century. The Holy Qur'an makes several references to covering for the sake of modesty (Qur'an 24:31) and relief from potential harassment (Qur'an 33:59). While the term "veiling" or *hijab*[53] is often associated with Muslim women, Qasim Rashid points out that the Holy Qur'an does not address women first on this matter: "It addresses men first. That's not a typo. Islam places the primary responsibility of observing *hijab* not on women – but on men. It's critical to understand this point" (Rashid 2017). The Holy Qur'an states:

> Tell the believing men that they should restrain their gaze (from looking at the women whom it is lawful for them to marry, and from others' private parts), and guard their private parts and chastity. This is what is purer for them. God is fully aware of all that they do (Qur'an 24:30).

Prophet Muhammad's own directives further affirm this view, as Rashid pointed out. The Prophet admonished men, "Be chaste yourselves, and women will be chaste as well."

The *burqa* – the article of clothing worn by some Muslim women around the world – has recently drawn attention in public and media spheres in relation to the position of women within the Islamic faith. Critics of the *burqa* claim that it represents a sign of oppression and denying Muslim women their basic human rights. I am not a woman and nor am I Muslim, but the controversy surrounding the *burqa* is problematic to me for several important reasons.[54]

I have strong feelings against any government setting specific demands on what women can and cannot wear. Forcing women to wear the *burqa* and denying women the right to wear one are two sides of the same coin in terms of oppression. Targeting and penalizing women for not wearing the *burqa*, or any veil for that matter, is unproductive in terms of our collective striving for equality. Though I may disagree with a woman who claims that their entire body must be covered in order for them to protect their honor, I will defend that woman's right to wear the *burqa* if she so wishes.

Banning the *burqa* outright – as countries like France have proposed – is an assault on the basic human right of women to control their own bodies and minds. Criminalizing this article of clothing is not, as some critics argue, a liberal or progressive policy that will help to achieve gender parity in "Western societies." Rather, banning the *burqa* is a form of bullying that forces Muslim women into abandoning a sacred tradition, a religious obligation, or a political expression.

My personal views on matters pertaining to the *burqa* and other forms of *hijab*[55] were significantly altered when I met Nicole Queen, a Texas native and self-proclaimed ex-party girl who converted to the Islamic faith in Dallas. Nicole explained to me that she, along with many other Muslim women, cover up to maintain their honor and modesty. For her, wearing the *abayah* provides self-confidence, as she explained: "[covering] made me feel like a nun who everyone respected because she lives her entire life for God, in the way she dresses. She isn't showing anything of her body. They can't look at you as a piece of meat."

Nicole Queen is not an isolated case. Many Muslim women around the world wear the *burqa* or other forms of Islamic veiling out of their own free will. This is a fact. Muslim women in France, for example, wear the *burqa* for a variety of political reasons including as a response to the overt "Westernization" of society and for freedom from male harassment. While it is true that some Muslim men may force their wives and daughters to dress in certain ways, Muslim women also employ their agency by abiding by their perceived obligation to conform to certain gender roles. Banning the *burqa* prevents Muslim women from exercising their human right to do what they want with their own bodies. They should be able to express themselves as they deem fit.

Singling out the *burqa* or other articles of clothing worn by Muslim women is a somber capitulation to the Islamophobic sentiment around the world. It is nothing short of oppressive to declare that a woman of a particular religious background cannot have the freedom over her body or personal expression.

Unfortunately, extremists on both sides of the isle are using the *burqa*, and subsequently Muslim women, in a virtual tug-of-war between civilizations. It is ironic that men who propose the banning of the *burqa* to "liberate" Muslim women act in a nearly identical way as men who propose laws that restrict a woman's right to do what she wishes with her own body and mind.

Banning the *burqa* also breaks Article 8 of the European Convention on Human Rights, a law implemented to protect and respect an individual's private life and legally safeguard a women's right to her personality and identity development. According to Articles 9 and 10 of the same legal text, all European women, regardless of religious background, have the right to freedom of expression. Further, Article 14 states that women should be protected from discrimination rooted in bigotry towards one's religious preferences or expressions.

Prophet Muhammad would be concerned about recent developments that put unnecessary hardship on the lives of Muslim women. In his Farewell Sermon Muhammad said to men, "Do treat your women well and be kind to them for they are your partners and committed helpers" (Appendix 2). Far from mistreating women, he actually liberated them. His life and legacy hold the key to extending freedom and compassion to them.

CHAPTER SIX

THE GOLDEN RULE

The so-called "Islamic civilization" and "Western civilization" are perceived by some scholars as mortal enemies that have been engaged in a war for religious supremacy, power, and territory since the 7th century. Following Muhammad's passing in 632, Christian scholars and leaders depicted him as a "false prophet," a charge that came across as inaccurate and insulting to Muslims. Christians also witnessed and directly experienced the expansion of the early Islamic state under the guidance of the caliphate into their Christian kingdoms. For some Christians, living under the *sharia* was a blessing in comparison to living under Byzantine rule. For other Christians, Islamic leadership posed a direct challenge to the idea of Christian supremacy.

Centuries after Muhammad's passing, the Crusades erupted and caused havoc in the Holy Land, an area which changed hands from Christians to Muslims (and vice versa) many times over. The rise of the Ottoman Empire also concerned European Christians, who stopped the Ottoman march westward at the "Gates of Vienna," a battle which is still noteworthy in the imagination of people who believe that Muslims are out to conquer the world, and in particular the present-day European Union.

We also cannot forget the 20th and 21st centuries, a period in history that has perhaps been the most challenging for Christian and Muslim relations. The countries of the so-called "Christian West" have invaded countless numbers of Muslim-majority countries around the world from Afghanistan, to Iraq, to Libya, invasions that have led to an alarming number of civilian deaths and the near destruction of entire countries. For Christians living around the world, the events of 9/11 and other terrorist attacks in the United States and European Union have only legitimized the clash of civilizations theory. All of these historical events have had a lasting impact on the development, or lack thereof, of Christian and Muslim relations.

Amidst the wars, violence, and defamatory language towards each other, Christians and Muslims – indeed all human beings – would be wise to remember that Jesus and Muhammad were kindred spirits who followed the Golden Rule.[56] The Golden Rule is the principle that "we should treat others as we would have them treat us."

Jesus and Muhammad both promoted peace in words and actions. During the Sermon on the Mount, Jesus spoke in front of a large crowd of people to preach the message of peace. One passage of the Sermon on the Mount reads: "Happy are those who work for peace; God will call them his children!" (Matthew 5:9). Peter, the first bishop of the Christian church, mirrored Jesus' teaching in his letter addressed to Christian refugees who were scattered throughout the northern part of Asia Minor.[57] In the face of the harsh conditions, Peter encouraged Christians to "love one another, and be kind and humble with one another. Do not pay back evil with evil or cursing with cursing; instead, pay back with a blessing, because a blessing is what God promised to give you when he called you" (Peter 3:8-9). Peter also told the Christians:

> If you want to enjoy life and wish to see good times, you must keep from speaking evil and stop telling lies. You must turn away from evil and do good; you must strive for peace with all your heart. For the Lord watches over the righteous and listens to their prayers; but he opposes those who do evil (1 Peter 3:10-12).

Prophet Muhammad also encouraged his followers to respect people of all faiths. It is noted in a *hadith* that Muhammad and several of the Companions were sitting down along a street in Medina. Suddenly a companion spotted a funeral procession approaching the group. In respect of the deceased soul, Muhammad stood as the procession crossed in front of him. At that moment, a companion, who was still sitting down, said to Muhammad: "This is the funeral of a Jewish person. He is not a Muslim." Upon hearing these words, Muhammad issued back, "Is he not a human soul?" (Considine 2016b).

"Respect all of humanity." That is the message that Muhammad was sending to his followers and Jewish neighbors.

The Yaqeen Institute for Islamic Research[58] noted in a *Huffington Post* article that Muhammad also prohibited harming others and focused on maintaining positive relationships with those who identify with other religious traditions:

> The Prophet Muhammad issued a stark warning about persecuting others, "Whoever harms a non-Muslim at peace with us will never smell the fragrance of paradise..." On the Day of Judgment, the Prophet himself will argue on behalf of persecuted non-Muslims and against the Muslims who persecuted them, "If anyone wrongs a non-Muslim at peace with us, violates his rights, burdens him with more work than he is able to do, or takes something from him without his consent, then I will be his advocate on the Day of Resurrection."

In summarizing these *hadith*s, the Yaqeen Institute researchers note: "This stunning indictment should make any Muslim think twice before hurting anyone."

Jesus and Muhammad also cared deeply about forgiveness. As a Christian myself, I ask God for forgiveness in my prayers by offering the following passage of the Lord's Prayer:

> "Our Father in heaven: May your holy name be honored; may your Kingdom come; may your will be done on earth as it is in heaven. Give us today the food we need. Forgive us the wrongs we have done, as we forgive the wrongs that others have done to us. Do not bring us to hard testing but keep us safe from the Evil One" (Matthew 6:9-13).

Likewise, after Muhammad marched into Mecca and conquered it without shedding a single drop of blood, he told his enemies, who had been torturing him and his followers for two decades, they were free to leave unharmed. He said to them:

"O Quraysh, what do you think that I am about to do with you?"

"Good. You are a noble brother, son of a noble brother."

"Go your way for you are the freed ones" (Guillaume 2017).

The Prophet forgave his enemies when they were at their weakest moment, even though they rose a number of times to fight him in battles, wounded and killed his friends and companions, and tried to assassinate him.

Muhammad's ability to forgive his enemies also captured the attention of Michael Wolfe, an American author and President of Unity Productions Foundation. Wolfe believed that Muhammad's most important teaching is forgiveness: "... [the Prophet] calls an end to revenge, to blood killing, to the vendetta, which has bled this culture terribly since he was born."[59]

Love for humanity is another principle seen in the teachings of Jesus and Muhammad. The Holy Bible states that Christians are to "honor all people" and "love the brotherhood" (1 Peter 2:17). Similarly, Paul's Letter to the Philippians living in Macedonia, written while Paul was in prison, encourages Christians to unite and love one another: "I urge you, then, to make me completely happy by having the same thoughts, sharing the same love, and being one in soul and mind" (Philippians 2:2).

Muhammad, on the other hand, stated: "All God's creatures are His family" (Al-Bayhaqi, Abu Nu'aym, Al-Tabarani) and added "None of you (truly believe) until he wishes for his brother what he wishes for himself" (Al-Bukhari).

Jesus and Muhammad encouraged human beings to speak kindly to each other and to avoid gossiping. Paul's Letter to the Ephesians, which focuses on unity for the whole of humanity, reflects Jesus' teachings in the following passages:

> Do not use harmful words, but only helpful words, the kind that build up and provide what is needed, so that what you say will do good to those who hear you... Get rid of all bitterness, passion, and anger. No more shouting or insults, no more hateful feelings of any sort. Instead, be kind and tenderhearted to one another, and forgive one another, as God has forgiven you through Christ (Ephesians 4:29; 31-32).

Similarly, Muhammad told his followers that "kindness is a mark of faith and whoever has not kindness has not faith" (Al-Bukhari).

Jihad in the Islamic and Christian traditions[60]

Critics of the Islamic faith frequently criticize *jihad* as a form of Islamic supremacism, oppression, and holy war against people who are not Muslim. Muslim extremists, on the other hand, similarly argue that *jihad* is an Islamic obligation calling on Muslims to use violence against minority populations living in Muslim societies. Viewing the term *jihad* through these frameworks alone exacerbates the deepening divide within the realm of our common humanity. A bit of clarity is therefore needed to demystify one of the most misunderstood terms in the realm of Islamic studies.

The term *jihad* is literally translated into the English language to mean "to struggle" or "to strive." A person that engages in *jihad* may be struggling in the face of personal struggles like fighting unhealthy addictions or striving to promote tolerance of diversity and love.

In terms of the relationship between *jihad* and war, Muslims are told to embark on military struggles for the purposes of self-defense. When asked by one of his companions, "What is the major *jihad*?" Muhammad replied: "The *jihad* of the self." The lesser *jihad*, he added, is engaging in war.

To be clear, the *sharia* allows the use of force, but only in matters of self-defense, and specifically in defense of those who are oppressed and unable to defend themselves. Scholar Niaz A. Shah adds the following clarification over the term:

> … the offensive theory of *jihad* is untenable. Muslim states follow the defensive theory of *jihad*. Islamic law also allows, under certain conditions, anticipatory self-defense. Only the head of a Muslim state (a ruler or caliph) is allowed to declare *jihad*. Most of the current so-called declarations of *jihad* have been issued by non-state actors, e.g. Al-Qaeda, who have no authority to declare *jihad*. These declarations thus have no validity under Islamic law and, indeed, Muslim states are fighting these armed groups. Islamic law imposes certain restrictions on the use of force in self-defense, i.e., military necessity,

distinction, and proportionality. Accepting an offer of peace and humanity are also relevant conditions (Shah 2013: 343).

While Muhammad condoned the use of violence, or the lesser *jihad*, in the context of self-defense and self-preservation, he cared more for the greater *jihad*. His approach on this matter is captured by William James Durant, a 20th century American historian and co-author of *The Story of Civilization*, in the following passage:

> If we judge greatness by influence, [Muhammad] was one of the giants of history. He undertook to raise the spiritual and moral level of people harassed into barbarism by heat and foodless wastes, and he succeeded more completely than any other reformer seldom has any man so fully realized his dream... When he began, Arabia was a desert flotsam of idolatrous tribes; when he died it was a nation.

Although the term *jihad* is not literally used in Christian scripture, the idea of struggling is at the very heart of Jesus's teachings. There are a number of instances in the New Testament that provide guidance for people who are struggling with problems or dilemmas in their lives. Here is a collection of verses on this matter:

> [Jesus said]: "Peace is what I leave with you; it is my own peace that I give you" (John 14:27).
>
> [Paul said to the Corinthians]: "Every test that you have experienced is the kind that normally comes to people. But God keeps his promise, and he will not allow you to be tested beyond your power to remain firm; at the time you are put to the test, he will give you the strength to endure it, and so provide you with a way out" (1 Corinthians 10:13).
>
> "My friends, consider yourselves fortunate when all kinds of trials come your way, for you know that when your faith succeeds in facing such trials, the result is the ability to endure. Make sure that your endurance carries you all the way without failing, so that you may be perfect and complete, lacking nothing" (James 1:2-4).
>
> [Paul said to the Romans]: "If someone has done you wrong, do not repay him with a wrong. Try to do what everyone considers to be good. Do everything possible on your part to live in peace with everybody. Never take revenge, my friends, but instead let God's anger

do it. For the scripture says, 'I will take revenge, I will pay back, says the Lord.' Instead, as the scripture says: 'If your enemies are hungry, feed them; if they are thirsty, give them a drink; for by doing this you will make them burn with shame.' Do not let evil defeat you; instead, conquer evil with good" (Romans 12:17-21).

[Paul said to the Corinthians]: "But [God's] answer was: 'My grace is all you need, for my power is greatest when you are weak.' I am most happy, then, to be proud of my weaknesses, in order to feel the protection of Christ's power over me. I am content with weaknesses, insults, hardships, persecutions, and difficulties for Christ's sake. For when I am weak, then I am strong" (2 Corinthians 12:9-10).

One major aspect of the "Christian *jihad*" is the practice of non-violence. When Roman soldiers arrested Jesus and brought him to Pontius Pilate, the Roman official governing Jerusalem, Jesus is said to have stated: "My kingdom does not belong to this world; if my kingdom belonged to this world, my followers would fight to keep me from being handed over to the Jewish authorities. No, my kingdom does not belong here!" (John 18: 36). Violence, as the passage highlights, is antithetical to Jesus's teachings.

In another moment of Jesus' life, when he was betrayed by Judas, one of the twelve disciples, Jesus was arrested by armed men. Peter, who was with Jesus, drew his sword and struck the Jewish High Priest's servant, cutting off his ear. Jesus said to his follower: "Put your sword back in its place. All who take the sword will die by the sword" (Matthew 26:52).

Similarly, the Islamic faith encourages Muslims to resist the temptation of taking up arms against enemies. The Holy Qur'an notes: "… If anyone slew a person unless it be for murder or for spreading mischief in the land it would be as if he slew the whole humanity: and if anyone saved a life it would be as if he saved the life of the whole humanity" (Qur'an 5:32). In another Qur'anic passage (2:190) Muslims are told to "Fight in the case of God those who start fighting you, but do not transgress limits (or start the attack); for God loveth not transgressors." It is clear that these two passages echo the Christian *jihad* of struggling in the name of non-violence.

The *jihad* of the Christian faith also calls on Christians to love all human beings. Jesus told his followers to "love your neighbor," but even more than that he told them to "Love your enemies, do good to those who hate you, bless those who curse you, and pray for those who mistreat you," according to the commandments documented in Luke (6:27). In a similar light, Romans (12:17-18) demands that Christians, even if wronged by someone, do everything possible to live in peace with everybody. Moreover, Paul encouraged the Christians of Rome to "always aim at those things that bring peace and that help strengthen one another" (Romans 14:19). Lastly, in Timothy (6:11-12), Paul inspired Christians to "Strive for righteousness, godliness, faith, love, endurance, and gentleness. Run your best in the race of faith, and win eternal life for yourself."

Peter, a contemporary of Paul's and the first bishop of the Church, echoed similar sentiments in a letter to a wide circle of early Christians:

> … do your best to add goodness to your faith; to your goodness add knowledge; to your knowledge add self-control; to your self-control add endurance; to your endurance add godliness; to your godliness add Christian affection; and to your Christian affection add love. These are the qualities you need, and if you have them in abundance, they will make you active and effective in your knowledge of our Lord Jesus Christ (Peter 2:5-7).

Peter's focus on doing good and searching for the truth mirrors the Holy Qur'an's emphasis on *ilm*, an Arabic term that translates to "knowledge." Similarly, Romans (12:1-2) urges human beings, in view of God's mercy, to not conform to the pattern of this world, "but let God transform you inwardly by a complete change of your mind. Then you will be able to know the will of God – what is good and is pleasing to him and is perfect."

Few religions in the world place as much emphasis on knowledge as the Islamic faith. The Holy Qur'an refers to knowledge more than 700 times. *Allah*, the Arabic for God, raises in rank those who have been given knowledge (Qur'an 58:11). Muhammad himself emphasized knowledge in a *hadith* in which he stated, "… seeking knowledge is a must for every Muslim, male or female, from cradle to grave in any part of the world." In another *hadith* he stated, "... the ink of the scholar is more sacred than the blood of the martyr."

The Qur'an also requires Muslims to search for ways of making peace. The holy book asks Muslims to leave others alone if they leave Muslim alone: "... refrain from fighting... and offer [them] peace, then God gives you no way to go against them" (Qur'an 4:9). Further, the Holy Qur'an states that Muslims are to speak well of others even if they are not believers of the Islamic faith: "... speak in a most kindly manner (unto those who do not share [your] beliefs)" (Qur'an 17:53-54). In addition, the Holy Qur'an also makes it clear that Muslims must not force others to believe in the Islamic faith: "... there is no compulsion in religion" (Qur'an 2:256).

Ultimately, Christians and Muslims are guided by their scripture to persevere in the face of personal and societal challenges. They are encouraged to struggle for the betterment of humanity in this life and to maintain steadfast belief in God in exchange for a higher reward when their lives on Earth inevitably end. Christians and Muslims indeed share a similar *jihad*, one of non-violence, love of humanity, the perfection of the soul, and the search for knowledge.

As noted at the beginning of the chapter, many critics today of the Islamic faith claim that the religion was "spread by the sword." As noted by Hugh Kennedy, author of *The Great Arab Conquest: How the Spread of Islam Changed the World We Live In*, "[t]he idea that Islam was spread, by the sword has had wide currency at many different times and the impression is still widespread among the less reflective sections of the media and the wider public that people converted to Islam because they were forced to do" (Kennedy n.d.: 1). Kennedy, however, concluded that Islamic civilization was not spread by the sword. These sentiments were echoed by Mohandas Ghandi, the "Father of the Nation" of India, who concluded after studying Muhammad's life that:

> "... it was not the sword that won a place for Islam... It was the rigid simplicity, the utter self-effacement of the Prophet, the scrupulous regard for pledges, his intense devotion to his friends and followers, his intrepidity, his fearlessness, his absolute trust in God and in his own

mission. These and not the sword carried everything before them and surmounted every obstacle."[61]

In other words, as Gandhi noted, it was the "greater *jihad*" that led to the spread and success of the Islamic faith during and after the life of Muhammad. This "greater *jihad*" is a struggle shared by Jesus, his disciples and apostles, as well as Christians living today.

Embracing the "Jihad of Jesus"[62]

"Our enemies are the Islamic faith and Muslims." These kind of words are oftentimes uttered by politicians, religious leaders, activists, or media personalities. Personally, I receive messages from Muslims who send me statements like, "Islam is superior to Christianity" and "Christianity is a false religion." Islamophobes and so-called "radical Muslims" appear to have similar motives – oppose and oppress those who do not share their worldviews, resort to violence to suppress other faith groups, and denounce the moral validity of people who do not think like they do. Now more than ever Christians and Muslims can benefit from a fresh understanding of their faith traditions and how these traditions may be able to build the much-needed bridges between these two populations.

David Andrews, an Australian citizen, interfaith activist, and author, provided this fresh understanding in his book *The Jihad of Jesus: The Sacred Nonviolent Struggle for Justice* (Wipf and Stock, 2015). Andrews believes that Christian and Muslim relations can be strengthened if both populations embrace the peaceful example of Jesus, which can subsequently help them unite peacefully to counter division, bigotry, and faith-based violence. His arguments are rooted in the idea that "… all people are loved, equally, by God, regardless of color, class, caste, or creed."

Despite his call for solidarity and peaceful coexistence between Christians and Muslims, Andrews acknowledges that there are theoretical differences between the Holy Qur'an and Holy Bible. These differences, however, are overshadowed by areas of "common ground." Actually, Andrews pushes the bar even further by saying that Christians and Muslims share "sacred ground" as rooted in their shared Abrahamic tradition.

The common, sacred ground that Andrews identifies is one exhibited by the *bismillah al-rahman al-rahim*, the Qur'anic phrase meaning "In the Name of God, the Merciful and Compassionate." Every chapter in the Qur'an, with the exception of one, starts with this phrase. The *bismillah* phrase is connected to the Christian faith through the kindness and humility of Jesus, a prophet in the Islamic tradition,[63] who Andrews thinks Christians should follow "with every beat of [their] hearts, through every vein in [their] head, and [their] hands, and [their] feet."

The *bismillah* spirit and Jesus's teachings directly challenge the dogmatic, judgmental, and intolerance of those Christians and Muslims who view the Islamic faith and the Christian tradition as fundamentally at odds with each other. Andrews prefers an open perspective to interreligious dialogue in the hope that it can lead to personal growth and transformational change in communities around the world. By engaging with one another in light of the *bismillah* spirit and Jesus's teachings, Christians and Muslims can transcend the ideology of religious supremacy.

The Jihad of Jesus reminds readers about the fragile state of our humanity and the disregard for human rights in our turbulent times. The time is ripe for Christians and Muslims to live the *bismillah* and channel their "inner-Jesus" by embracing non-violence and struggling for peace in our world. This is the shared *jihad* for Christians and Muslims.

An unlikely connection between Muhammad and Washington[64]

"The best among you," Muhammad said to his followers, "are those who have the best manners and character." More than 1,100 years after he shared these words, Muhammad's wisdom would be echoed again, but this time in the British colony of Virginia by a 13-year-old schoolboy who started writing down a set of behavioral rules to be published later as the book *Rules of Civility*. The schoolboy was none other than George Washington, who would later become the first president of the United States of America.

Muhammad and Washington may seem like an unlikely connection, but in fact they share similar biographies. They were both students of history, restorers of justice, and had to fight for their freedoms. They both led their respective nations through successful revolutions. Both men united a large amount of territory and served as the founding father of two nations – the *ummah* and the United States of America.

The connection between Muhammad and Washington can be explored in the Holy Qur'an, which documents God's revelations to Muhammad, and *Rules of Civility*, which is less concerned with religious affairs and focuses more on social rules and norms. The Qur'an and *Rules of Civility* have different frames, but both texts – in a wider sense – offer guidance toward achieving a more peaceful and noble life.

Muhammad and Washington advised their peers to keep their mouths free of foul language. In the Holy Qur'an, offensive name-calling is forbidden: "O you who believe! Let not some people among you deride another people... Nor defame one another; nor insult one another with nicknames. Evil is using names with vile meaning after (those so addressed have accepted) the faith" (Qur'an 49:11). In *Rules of Civility* (Rule #49), Washington said: "[u]se no reproachful language against anyone, neither curse nor revile." He added in Rule #65: "[s]peak not injurious words, neither in jest nor earnest" and "[s]coff at no one, although they give occasion."

In regards to how Muslims should respond to divisive and inflammatory remarks or events as guided by Muhammad, consider the following two stories.

"[U.S.] Marine hosts 'Draw Muhammad' protest outside mosque." I read this news headline following a national story that caused a stir in 2015. John Ritzheimer, a self-professed "American patriot," organized this event in order to, as he explained it, protect the U.S. Constitution's First Amendment right of freedom of speech. Many critics, however, saw the event as nothing more than an anti-Islamic and anti-Muslim gathering. Ritzheimer's protest outside of the Islamic Community Center in northwest Phoenix, Arizona was inspired by another cartoon contest several weeks earlier in Garland, Texas.

How would Muhammad respond to events like those held in Phoenix and Garland?

First, Muhammad would recommend that people respond to any kind of insult by remaining calm and respectful. Muhammad was insulted and attacked regularly by the people closest to him, as well as his enemies. The Islamic sources relate that pagans of Mecca used to throw waste and trash on Muhammad's doorstep. The kind of waste or trash in the 7th century was not the kind of waste or trash we think of in the 21st century. Instead of seeing plastic scraps or newspapers, Muhammad saw food scraps and likely even slaughtered animals. Imam Al-Suhayli[65] relates one of the stories in his commentary on the *seerah* of ibn Hashim, called "Al-Raud Al-Anif":

> The Chapter on [the Harms and Abuse] that the Messenger of Allah (Allah's peace and blessings be upon him) received from His People: Ibn Ishaq, Al-Waqidi, Al-Taymi, Ibn 'Uqbah and others mention under this chapter many incidents...
>
> ... from throwing sand on his [blessed] head... and from amongst [the incidents] is that they would pile up torn intestines, human feces and blood on his door, and through a dead sheep's uterus into his cooking pot" (Al-Raud Al-Anif, Al-Suhayli).
>
> Ibn Sa'd, the early biographer and historian, narrated in his work on history, Al-Tabaqat, through 'Aisha that the Prophet (peace be upon him) was reported to have said,
>
> "I was [living, in Mecca] between the two worst neighbors [one could have]: between Abu Lahab [his uncle and sworn enemy] and 'Uqbah Ibn Abi M'uayt [who once threw a sheep's insides on his blessed head, peace be upon him, while he was praying]. Indeed, they would come with bloodied intestines and throw it on my doorstep..." (Al-Tabaqa, Ibn Sa'id, as quoted in Suyuti's Jami' Al-Kabir).

Instead of reacting aggressively or angrily, Muhammad showed compassion and forgiveness. He understood the value of staying silent in light of situations that may cause anger inside of an individual. "If any of you become angry," he said, "let him keep silent." Muhammad's ability to maintain self-control is an exemplary model, especially in today's times when Christians often hurl insults at Muslims (and vice versa).

Indeed, Muhammad and Washington taught their peers to improve relations with others by using kindness and positive words.

Both men hoped that using civil language would help groups avoid misunderstandings and create a more harmonious society.

In addition to kindness, the theme of modesty pops up many times in the Islamic holy text. For example, the Holy Qur'an states: "Tell the believing men to lower their gaze and to be mindful of their chastity; in this they will be more considerate for their own well-being and purity" (Qur'an 24:30-31). Further, the Holy Qur'an requests that women "not display the charms of their bodies beyond what may be apparent thereof; hence, let them draw their head-coverings over their bosoms" (Qur'an 24:31).

Washington also wrote about the importance of modest appearances. Rule #52 notes: "In your apparel, be modest and endeavor to accommodate nature rather than to procure admiration." Rule #52 adds: "Keep to the fashion of your equals, such as are civil and orderly, with respect to times and places."

Muhammad and Washington encouraged their peers to dress appropriately because a modest and clean appearance is an indication of healthy inner feelings and humble attitudes.

Muhammad and Washington also believe in the virtue of humility. The Holy Qur'an (25:63) states that "[t]he servants of the Merciful are those who walk on the earth in humility" and that the "[s]uccessful indeed are the believers who humble themselves in their prayers" (Qur'an 23:02). The Islamic tradition even has a term – *ujb* – which warns human beings on the dangers of arrogance and exaggerating one's personal accomplishments. Comparatively, Washington noted in Rule #63 that "a man ought not to value himself of his achievements or rare qualities, his riches, his titles, his virtue or his kindred."

The humility of Muhammad and Washington was crucial to the success of their fledgling nations in the 7th and 18th centuries respectively. The direction of the *ummah* and the United States of America would have been much different if these two men were selfish, egotistical, and presumptuous leaders.

Following humility, respect also is mentioned in the Holy Qur'an and *Rules of Civility*, especially as it pertains to respecting one's parents. The Holy Qur'an (17:23-24) calls for "good treatment" of parents : "Whether one or both of them reach old age [while] with you, say not to them [so much as] 'oof [i.e., an expression of irritation] and do not repel them but speak to them a noble word." Washington, on the other hand, stated in Rule #108 that people should "[h]onor and obey" their parents "although they may be poor."

While it may appear as an obscure similarity, Muhammad and Washington also cared a great deal about good hygiene. The Holy Qur'an (5:6) states that God calls on people to keep themselves pure and clean, especially before praying: "When you rise up for the Prayer, (if you have no ablution) wash your faces and your hands up to (and including) the elbows, and lightly rub your heads (with water), and (wash) your feet up to (and including) the ankles." Similarly, in *Rules of Civility*, Washington explained in Rule #15 that people should keep their "nails clean and short," and their "hands and teeth clean, yet without showing any concern for them." He added that people should wear clean clothing in Rule #51: "Wear not your clothes foul, ripped or dusty… and take heed that you approach not to any uncleanness." Both men stressed the importance of maintaining a clean, well-presented physical appearance, because they believed that good hygiene was a projection of positive body images and healthy minds.

Ultimately, Muhammad and Washington were gentlemen of the highest degree. This description is evident in the connections between the Holy Qur'an and *Rules of Civility*. Perhaps it is therefore no surprise that Muslims worldwide see Muhammad as the perfect human being. With that said, perhaps it is surprising that even non-Muslims have praised the Prophet. In his pamphlet *Muhammad: The Prophet of Islam*, K.S. Rao said that Muhammad is the perfect model for human life.

In a similar fashion, Washington's contemporary, Richard Henry Lee, once said that he was "first in war, first in peace, and first in the hearts of his countrymen." Even Washington's nemesis, King George III of the United Kingdom of Great Britain, said that Washington was "placed in a light the most distinguished of any man living" and had "the greatest character of his age."

Perhaps Christians and Muslims worldwide can forge better relations with each other if they followed the advice that Muhammad and Washington provided.

In summary, Muhammad was much like Jesus in the sense that he abided by the "Golden Rule." Muhammad and Jesus taught their followers to "treat others as you wish to be treated." One of Muhammad's favorite sayings was: "Forgive him who wrongs you, join him who cuts you off, do good to him who does evil to you." The Prophet believed that keeping good relations between people was a fundamental component of Muslim identity, because quarrels and bad feelings destroy mankind. As Muhammad stated: "Do you know what is better than charity, fasting, and prayer? It is keeping peace and good relations among people, as quarrels and bad feelings destroy mankind."[66]

Imagine what the world could be like if all human beings heeded his noble call.

CONCLUSION: THE SPIRIT OF TRUTH

A s an advocate for interreligious dialogue between Christians
and Muslims, and indeed between all human beings, I am
often faced with the question of whether I am a Muslim, or
if I am interested in converting to the Islamic faith. On any given
day I may be asked, "Why don't you convert if you admire Prophet
Muhammad so much?" or "Do you accept Muhammad as the seal
of the prophets?"

For some Muslims, my love of Muhammad is not enough. Some
Muslims request that I take the concrete steps of conversion by taking the *shahada* and devoting myself to the Five Daily Prayers. For
these people, converting to the Islamic faith is the only way that I can
be a "true believer" who would be saved from the hellfire.

"How can a Christian accept Muhammad as one of God's prophets?" they ask.

I often have in-person and online interactions with Muslims
who appear to be genuinely frustrated, and perhaps even angered,
that I do not define myself as a Muslim. On one occasion, a young
Muslim man tweeted me the following passage from the Holy
Qur'an (3:85): "And whosoever desires a religion other than Islam,
it shall not be accepted from him, and in the hereafter, he shall be
one of the losers." The person then sent me a follow-up message
that read: "My ultimate success as a Muslim is saving you from
the hellfire so that you may be admitted to paradise by the mercy
of God." As you may imagine, I was a bit startled by this message
about the so-called doomed fate of Christians according to the
Holy Qur'an.

But, if the preceding chapters showed one thing, it is that Muhammad did not condemn Christians to the eternal hellfire. Nor did
the Prophet think that Christians are inferior people who have no
chance of making it to heaven. Far from these claims, Muhammad's
admiration for Christians and the Christian faith is clear in his in-

teractions with the Christians of Najran and the Covenants with the Christians of his time. His admiration also is clear in his views on the King of Abyssinia. Additionally, Muhammad's positive views on Jews and Judaism is evident in the Constitution of Medina, and his admirable positions on racial equality are evident in his relationship with Bilal as well as his Farewell Sermon.

One of the reoccurring terms that appeared throughout this book is *ahl al-kitab*, or "People of the Book." The Holy Qur'an provides Jews, Christians, and Muslims with this honorable title that effectively unites monotheistic believers into a "super-religion," or perhaps we should call it a "super-tribe." In terms of Christians specifically, the Holy Qur'an (3:114) describes Christians as "among the righteous" and the book even goes as far as stating that the people whose faith is closest to the beliefs of Muslims are "those who say, 'We are Christians'" (Qur'an 5:82).

Far from viewing Christians as inferior, Muhammad actually revered them because of their belief in God, the Day of Judgment, and doing good deeds as commanded by Jesus. The Prophet considered Christians to be more like family members and allies rather than adversaries and enemies.

Some Christians, on the other hand, have referred to me as a heretic or pseudo-Christian because I publicly recognize Muhammad as a prophet. According to popular arguments, Christians who recognize Muhammad's prophethood are at risk of blaspheming.

Perhaps, however, the Bible actually recognizes Muhammad's prophethood. Consider John (14:15-17), or what is popularly referred to as the "spirit of truth" verse. Some Christians and Muslims turn to this Gospel passage in either justifying Muhammad's prophethood or legitimizing Jesus's prediction that another prophet (i.e. Muhammad) would follow him. In this verse Jesus states that he will "ask the Father, and he will give you another Helper, who will stay with you forever. He is the Spirit, who reveals the truth about God." Jesus goes on to say: "The world cannot receive him, because it cannot see him or know him. But you know him, because he remains with you and is in you."

I am by no means the first Christian or "non-Muslim" to recognize Muhammad as a prophet. There is in fact a long list of leaders throughout history that have praised the life and legacy of the Prophet. Michael H. Hart, author of *The 100: A Ranking of the Most Influential Persons in History*[67] ranked Muhammad as the most influential person in the history of the world. Hart wrote the following: "My choice of Muhammad to lead the list of the world's most influential persons may surprise some readers and may be questioned by others, but he was the only man in history who was supremely successful on both the religious and secular levels" (Hart 1978: 33). Hart further broke down his explanation by identifying several key themes as outlined in the following passage:

> First, Muhammad played a far more important role in the development of Islam than Jesus did in the development of the Christian faith. Although Jesus was responsible for the main ethical and moral precepts of Christianity (insofar as these differed from Judaism), it was St. Paul who was the main developer of Christian theology, its principal prose-lytizer, and the author of a large portion of the New Testament.
>
> Muhammad, however, was responsible for both the theology of Islam and its main ethical and moral principles. In addition, he played the key role in proselytizing the new faith, and in establishing the religious practices of Islam. Moreover, he is the author of the Moslem holy scriptures, the Koran, a collection of Muhammad's statements that he believed had been divinely inspired. Most of these utterances were copied more or less faithfully during Muhammad's lifetime and were collected together in authoritative from not long after his death. The Qur'an, therefore, closely represents Muhammad's ideas and teachings and, to a considerable extent, his exact words. No such detailed compilation of the teachings of Christ has survived. Since the Koran is at least as important to Moslems as the Bible is to Christians, the influence of Muhammad through the medium of the Koran has been enormous. It is probably that the relative influence of Muhammad on Islam has been larger than the combined influence of Jesus Christ and St. Paul on the Christian faith. On the purely religious level, then, it seems likely that Muhammad has been as influential in human history as Jesus.
>
> Furthermore, Muhammad (unlike Jesus) was a secular as well as a religious leader. In fact, as the driving force behind the Arab con-

quests, he may well rank as the most influential political leader of all time… It is this unparalleled combination of secular and religious influence which I feel entitles Muhammad to be considered the most influential single figure in human history (Hart 1978: 9-10).

Hart's description of Muhammad is fitting considering that the Prophet wore many hats and filled many roles throughout the course of his life. Indeed, Muhammad was not merely a prophet of God. While we should of course not dismiss the importance of his prophetic example and message, it is worth remembering that he was also a revolutionary, statesman, army general, jurist, lawgiver, social activist, community leader, businessman, friend, husband, father, son, and even an orphan in his youth.

Furthermore, K.S. Ramakrishna Rao, a professor of philosophy at the University of Mysore in India, praised Muhammad because of how successfully he played the various roles in his life:

> There is Mohammad the Prophet, there is Mohammad the General; Mohammad the Warrior; Mohammad the Businessman; Mohammad the Preacher; Mohammad the Philosopher; Mohammad the Statesman; Mohammad the Orator; Mohammad the reformer; Mohammad the Refuge of orphans; Mohammad the Protector of slaves; Mohammad the Emancipator of women; Mohammad the Law-giver; Mohammad the Judge; Mohammad the Saint. And in all these magnificent roles, in all these departments of human activities, he is like, a hero… .[68]

Thomas Carlyle, the Scottish author and historian during the Victorian era, similarly characterized Muhammad as "tolerant, kind, cheerful and praiseworthy and perhaps he would joke and tease his companions. He was just, truthful, smart, pure, magnanimous and present-minded."

Annie Besant, an 18th and 19th century British social reformer and campaigner for women's rights, noted that: "It is impossible for anyone who studies the personality of the great Prophet of the Arabs, and come to know how this prophet used to live, and how he taught the people, but to feel respect towards this honorable prophet; one of the great messengers whom Allah sent."

Like Besant and those listed before her, I also consider Muhammad to be a prophet. The term "prophet" is certainly open for interpretation, and thus has a varied meaning. I define a prophet as a person who inspires human beings to strive closer to God. A prophet is a human being who has extraordinary insight and intuition into the mysteries of our existence, as well as the purpose of life itself. A prophet is a messenger of God that brings human beings to a higher state of being. A prophet is someone who works on earth to foster peace and justice to communities that need both. A prophet is a person who is sensitive to the well-being of other people regardless of their cultural, ethnic, religious, or racial identities. A prophet also cares about humanity more than tribe or creed.

Nevertheless, my recognition of Muhammad as a prophet does not mean that I consider him to be the final prophet or "seal of the prophets," as many Muslims worldwide tend to believe. This kind of classification, in my opinion, is too restrictive. I believe that God will continue to send prophets to Earth so long as human beings are living on the planet.

I also do not necessarily believe in everything that Muhammad said or did according to the Holy Qur'an and *Hadith*, but I also do not believe in everything that Jesus or Moses said or did according to the Bible either. I accept aspects of the various Abrahamic traditions and believe that all of them provided equally valuable and truthful messages.

Final words

This book sought out to counter extremism in an age of extremism. Extremist movements, whether they are rooted in religious superiority or racial supremacy, are mundane movements that dull the human spirit and divide human beings along ideological lines. At their core, extremist ideologies prevent human beings as a collective from maximizing their potential and reaching the states of peace and justice. Extremism in its varied forms also isolates human beings from our common humanity.

Prophet Muhammad was by no means an extremist in these senses. Quite the opposite, he was an "extremist" in the sense that he cared deeply for – and loved – his fellow human beings. He embarked upon a life of "radical love" that embraced the destitute, orphans, racial and religious minorities, and all other human beings who had previously been excluded from participating in and contributing to the betterment of society.

Muhammad's pluralistic vision for his *ummah*, and indeed the world at large, is timely considering the levels of extremism worldwide, particularly as they pertain to the persecution of Christians and other minority populations in Muslim-majority countries. Let me also remind Christian readers around the world that they would be wise to follow Muhammad's pluralistic and civic ethos in terms of their relations with Muslims.

Muhammad's engagement with humanity can serve as a tool to counter our age of extremism. His interactions with his fellow human beings and his teachings on equality are antithetical to popular stereotypes that the Islamic faith is inherently "anti-Christian," and that Muhammad is a "crazed warlord." The life and legacy of the Prophet remind us all about the possibilities for human beings, especially Jews and Christians, to live side-by-side in peace and harmony.

APPENDIX 1 – THE CONSTITUTION OF MEDINA

The following translation of the Constitution of Medina was created by Muhammad Hamidullah, a Muslim scholar, based on several historical sources including the Seerah of Ibn Hisham, the Seerah of Ibn Ishaq, *Kitab-Al-Amwal* by Abu Ubaid, and *Al-Bidayah-wan-Nihaya* by Ibn Kathir. Hamidullah's translation is found in his book *The First Written Constitution of the World: An Important Document of the Prophet's Time* (1975).

A Translation of the Constitution of the City-State of Madina in the Time of the Prophet (صلى الله عليه وسلم)

Hamidullah's note: [I have tried to make the translation very clear so as not to require any marginal notes for its understanding. The clauses have been numbered, to facilitate easy reference. Since this numbering has been agreed upon and is the same in Germany, Holland, Italy and other places, so whenever I have had to differ I have indicated my difference by subdividing the clause into (a), (b), etc., so as not to interfere with the international numbering.]

In the name of God, the Beneficent and the Merciful

(1) This is a prescript of Muhammad (صلى الله عليه وسلم), the Prophet and Messenger of God (to operate) between the faithful and the followers of Islam from among the Quraish and the people of Madina and those who may be under them, may join them and take part in wars in their company.

(2) They shall constitute a separate political unit (Ummat [or *ummah*]) as distinguished from all the people (of the world).

(3) The emigrants from the Quraish shall be (responsible) for their own ward; and shall pay their blood-money in mutual collaboration and shall secure the release of their own prisoners by paying

their ransom from themselves, so that the mutual dealings between
the believers be in accordance with the principles of goodness and
justice.

(4) And Banu 'Awf shall be responsible for their own ward and
shall pay their blood-money in mutual collaboration, and every
group shall secure the release of its own prisoners by paying their
ransom from themselves so that the dealings between the believers
be in accordance with the principles of goodness and justice.

(5) And Banu Al-Harith-ibn-Khazraj shall be responsible for
their own ward and shall pay their blood-money in mutual collaboration and every group shall secure the release of its own prisoners
by paying their ransom from themselves, so that the dealings between the believers be in accordance with the principles of goodness
and justice.

(6) And Banu Sa'ida shall be responsible for their own ward,
and shall pay their blood-money in mutual collaboration and every
group shall secure the release of its own prisoners by paying their
ransom from themselves, so that the dealings between the believers
be in accordance with the principles of goodness and justice.

(7) And Banu Jusham shall be responsible for their own ward
and shall pay their blood-money in mutual collaboration and every
group shall secure the release of its own prisoners by paying their
ransom so that the dealings between the believers be in accordance
with the principles of goodness and justice.

(8) And Banu an-Najjar shall be responsible for their own ward
and shall pay their blood-money in mutual collaboration and every
group shall secure the release of its own prisoners by paying their
ransom so that the dealings between the believers be in accordance
with the principles of goodness and justice.

(9) And Banu 'Amr-ibn-'Awf shall be responsible for their own
ward and shall pay their blood-money in mutual collaboration and
every group shall secure the release of its own prisoners by paying
their ransom, so that the dealings between the believers be in accordance with the principles of goodness and justice.

(10) And Banu-al-Nabit shall be responsible for their own ward
and shall pay their blood-money in mutual collaboration and every

group shall secure the release of its own prisoners by paying their ransom so that the dealings between the believers be in accordance with the principles of goodness and justice.

(11) And Banu-al-Aws shall be responsible for their own ward and shall pay their blood-money in mutual collaboration and every group shall secure the release of its own prisoners by paying their ransom, so that the dealings between the believers be in accordance with the principles of goodness and justice.

(12) (a) And the believers shall not leave any one, hard-pressed with debts, without affording him some relief, in order that the dealings between the believers be in accordance with the principles of goodness and justice. (b) Also no believer shall enter into a contract of clientage with one who is already in such a contract with another believer.

(13) And the hands of pious believers shall be raised against every such person as rises in rebellion or attempts to acquire anything by force or is guilty of any sin or excess or attempts to spread mischief among the believers ; their hands shall be raised all together against such a person, even if he be a son to any one of them.

(14) And no believer shall kill another believer in retaliation for an unbeliever, nor shall he help an unbeliever against a believer.

(15) And the protection of God is one. The humblest of them (believers) can, by extending his pro-tection to any one, put the obligation on all; and the believers are brothers to one another as against all the people (of the world).

(16) And that those who will obey us among the Jews, will have help and equality. Neither shall they be oppressed nor will any help be given against them.

(17) And the peace of the believers shall be one. If there be any war in the way of God, no believer shall be under any peace (with the enemy) apart from other believers, unless it (this peace) be the same and equally binding on all.

(18) And all those detachments that will fight on our side will be relieved by turns.

(19) And the believers as a body shall take blood vengeance in the way of God.

(20) (a) And undoubtedly pious believers are the best and in the rightest course. (b) And that no associator (non-Muslim subject) shall give any protection to the life and property of a Quraishite, nor shall he come in the way of any believer in this matter.

(21) And if any one intentionally murders a believer, and it is proved, he shall be killed in retaliation, unless the heir of the murdered person be satisfied with blood-money. And all believers shall actually stand for this ordinance and nothing else shall be proper for them to do.

(22) And it shall not be lawful for any one, who has agreed to carry out the provisions laid down in this code and has affixed his faith in God and the Day of Judgment, to give help or protection to any murderer, and if he gives any help or protection to such a person, God's curse and wrath shall be on him on the Day of Resurrection, and no money or compensation shall be accepted from such a person.

(23) And that whenever you differ about anything, refer it to God and to Muhammad (صلى الله عليه وسلم).

(24) And the Jews shall share with the believers the expenses of war so long as they fight in conjunction,

(25) And the Jews of Banu 'Awf shall be considered as one political community (Ummat) along with the believers—for the Jews their religion, and for the Muslims theirs, be one client or patron. He, however, who is guilty of oppression or breach of treaty, shall suffer the resultant trouble as also his family, but no one besides.

(26) And the Jews of Banu-an-Najjar shall have the same rights as the Jews of Banu 'Awf.

(27) And the Jews of Banu-al-Harith shall have the same rights as the Jews of Banu 'Awf.

(28) And the Jews of Banu Sa'ida shall have the same rights as the Jews of Banu 'Awf.

(29) And the Jews of Banu Jusham shall have the same rights as the Jews of Banu 'Awf.

(30) And the Jews of Banu al-Aws shall have the same rights as the Jews of Banu 'Awf.

(31) And the Jews of Banu Tha'laba shall have the same rights as the Jews of Banu 'Awf. Of course, whoever is found guilty of oppres-

sion or violation of treaty, shall himself suffer the consequent trouble as also his family, but no one besides.

(32) And Jafna, who are a branch of the Tha'laba tribe, shall have the same rights as the mother tribes.

(33) And Banu-ash-Shutaiba shall have the same rights as the Jews of Banu 'Awf; and they shall be faithful to, and not violators of, treaty.

(34) And the mawlas (clients) of Tha'laba shall have the same rights as those of the original members of it.

(35) And the sub-branches of the Jewish tribes shall have the same rights as the mother tribes.

(36) (a) And that none of them shall go out to fight as a soldier of the Muslim army, without the per-mission of Muhammad (صلى الله عليه وسلم). (b) And no obstruction shall be placed in the way of any one"s retaliation for beating or injuries; and whoever sheds blood shall be personally responsible for it as well as his family; or else (i.e., any step beyond this) will be of oppression; and God will be with him who will most faithfully follow this code (sahifdh) in action.

(37) (a) And the Jews shall bear the burden of their expenses and the Muslims theirs. (b) And if any one fights against the people of this code, their (i.e., of the Jews and Muslims) mutual help shall come into operation, and there shall be friendly counsel and sincere behaviour between them; and faithfulness and no breach of covenant.

(38) And the Jews shall be bearing their own expenses so long as they shall be fighting in conjunction with the believers.

(39) And the Valley of Yathrib (Madina) shall be a Haram (sacred place) for the people of this code.

(40) The clients (mawla) shall have the same treatment as the original persons (i.e., persons accepting clientage). He shall neither be harmed nor shall he himself break the covenant.

(41) And no refuge shall be given to any one without the permission of the people of the place (i.e., the refugee shall have no right of giving refuge to others).

(42) And that if any murder or quarrel takes place among the people of this code, from which any trouble may be feared, it shall be referred to God and God's Messenger, Muhammad (صلى الله عليه وسلم)

; and God will be with him who will be most particular about what is written in this code and act on it most faithfully.

(43) The Quraish shall be given no protection nor shall they who help them.

(44) And they (i.e., Jews and Muslims) shall have each other's help in the event of any one invading Yathrib.

(45) (a) And if they (i.e., the Jews) are invited to any peace, they also shall offer peace and shall be a party to it; and if they invite the believers to some such affairs, it shall be their (Muslims) duty as well to reciprocate the dealings, excepting that any one makes a religious war. (b) On every group shall rest the responsibility of (repulsing) the enemy from the place which faces its part of the city.

(46) And the Jews of the tribe of al-Aws, clients as well as original members, shall have the same rights as the people of this code: and shall behave sincerely and faithfully towards the latter, not perpetrating any breach of covenant. As one shall sow so shall he reap. And God is with him who will most sincerely and faithfully carry out the provisions of this code.

(47) And this prescript shall not be of any avail to any oppressor or breaker of covenant. And one shall have security whether one goes out to a campaign or remains in Madina, or else it will be an oppression and breach of covenant. And God is the Protector of him who performs the obligations with faithfulness and care, as also His Messenger Muhammad (صلى الله عليه وسلم).

Appendix 2 – The Farewell Sermon

The Farewell Sermon (also referred to as the Last Sermon or Final Sermon) of Prophet Muhammad was delivered after the *ummah* completed the *hajj*, the pilgrimage to Mecca. Ibn Hisham offers the following version of the Sermon. It has been translated into English.

"The Final Sermon"

O People, lend me an attentive ear, for I know not whether after this year, I shall ever be amongst you again. Therefore, listen to what I am saying to you very carefully and take these words to those who could not be present here today.

O People, just as you regard this month, this day, this city as Sacred, so regard the life and property of each other as sacred. Return the goods entrusted to you to their rightful owners. Hurt no one so that no one may hurt you. Remember that you will indeed meet your Lord, and that He will indeed reckon your deeds. God has forbidden you to take interest, therefore all interest obligation shall henceforth be waived. Your capital, however, is yours to keep. You will neither inflict nor suffer any inequity. God has judged that there shall be no interest, and that all the interest due to Abbas Ibn Abd'al Muttalib[69] shall henceforth be waived.

Beware of Satan, for the safety of your religion. He has lost all hope that he will ever be able to lead you astray in big things, so beware of following him in small things.

O People, it is true that you have certain rights with regard to your women, but they also have rights over you. Remember that you have taken them as your wives only under a trust from God and with His permission. If they abide by your right then to them belongs the right to be fed and clothed in kindness. Do treat your women well and be kind to them for they are your partners and committed helpers. And it is your right that they do not make friends with any one of whom you do not approve, as well as never to be unchaste.

O People, listen to me in earnest, worship God, perform your five daily prayers, fast during the month of Ramadan, and offer *zakat*. Perform *hajj* if you have the means.

All mankind is from Adam and Eve. An Arab has no superiority over a non-Arab, nor does a non-Arab have any superiority over an Arab; white has no superiority over black, nor does a black have any superiority over white; [none have any superiority over another] except by piety and good action. Learn that every Muslim is a brother to every Muslim and that the Muslims constitute one brotherhood. Nothing shall be legitimate to a Muslim which belongs to a fellow Muslim unless it was given freely and willingly. Do not, therefore, do injustice to yourselves.

Remember, one day you will appear before God and answer for your deeds. So beware, do not stray from the path of righteousness after I am gone.

O People, no prophet or apostle will come after me, and no new faith will be born. Reason well, therefore, O People, and understand the words which I convey to you. I leave behind me two things, the Holy Qur'an and my example, the Sunnah, and if you follow these you will never go astray.

All those who listen to me shall pass on my words to others and those to others again; and it may be that the last ones understand my words better than those who listen to me directly. Be my witness, O God, that I have conveyed your message to your people.

"This day I have perfected your religion for you, completed my grace upon you, and have chosen Islam for you as your religion" (Qur'an 5:3).

Appendix 3 – The Covenant with the Monks of Mount Sinai

The following text of the Covenant of the Prophet Muhammad with the Monks of Mount Sinai was created by the Prophet Muhammad and translated by John Andrew Morrow. The translation is found in *Six Covenants of the Prophet Muhammad with the Christians of His Time: The Primary Documents*, edited by John A. Morrow.

In the Name of Allah, the Most Compassionate, the Most Merciful

(A copy of the manuscript of the covenant written by Muhammad, the son of 'Abd Allah, may the peace and blessings of Allah be upon him, to all the Christians).

This covenant was written by Muhammad, the son of 'Abd Allah, the proclaimer and warner, trusted to protect Allah's creations, in order that people may raise no claim against Allah after [the advent of] His Messengers for Allah is Almighty, Wise.

He has written it for the members of his religion and to all those who profess the Christian religion in East and West, near or far, Arabs or non-Arabs, known or unknown, as a covenant of protection.

If anyone breaks the covenant herein proclaimed, or contravenes or transgresses its commands, he has broken the Covenant of Allah, breaks his bond, makes a mockery of his religion, deserves the curse [of Allah], whether he is a sultan or another among the believing Muslims.

If a monk or pilgrim seeks protection, in mountain or valley, in a cave or in tilled fields, in the plain, in the desert or in a church, I am behind them, defending them from every enemy; I, my helpers, all the members of my religion, and all my followers, for they [the monks and the pilgrims] are my proteges and my subjects.

I protect them from interference with their supplies and from the payment of taxes save what they willingly renounce. There shall be no compulsion or constraint against them in any of these matters.

A bishop shall not be removed from his bishopric, nor a monk from his monastery, nor a hermit from his tower, nor shall a pilgrim be hindered from his pilgrimage. Moreover, no building from among their churches shall be destroyed, nor shall the money from their churches be used for the building of mosques or houses for the Muslims. Whoever does such a thing violates Allah's covenant and dissents from the Messenger of Allah.

Neither poll-tax nor fees shall be laid on monks, bishops, or worshippers for I protect them, wherever they may be, on land or sea, in East and West, in North and South. They are under my protection within my covenant, and under my security, against all harm.

Those who also isolate themselves in the mountains or in sacred sites shall be free from the poll-tax, land tribute and from tithe or duty on whatever they grow for their own use, and they shall be assisted in raising a crop by a free allowed of one *qadah* [unit of dry measure] in every *ard-abb* [= 6 *wayba* = 24 *rub'a*] for their personal use.

They shall not be obliged to serve in war, or to pay the poll-tax; even those for whom an obligation to pay land tribute exists, or who possess resources in land or from commercial activity, shall not have to pay more than twelve *dirham*s a head per year.

On no one shall an unjust tax be imposed, and with the People of the Book there is to be no strife, unless it be over what is for the good [Holy Qur'an 29:46]. We wish to take them under the wing of our mercy, and the penalty of vexation shall be kept at a distance from them, wherever they are and wherever they may settle.

If a Christian woman enters a Muslim household, she shall be received with kindness, and she shall be given opportunity to pray in her church; there shall be no dispute between her and a man who loves her religion. Whoever contravenes the covenant of Allah and acts to the contrary is a rebel against his covenant and his Messenger.

These people shall be assisted in the maintenance of their religious buildings and their dwellings; thus they will be aided in their faith and kept true to their allegiance.

None of them shall be compelled to bear arms, but the Muslims shall defend them; and they shall never contravene this promise of protection until the house comes and the world ends.

As witness to this covenant, which was written by Muhammad, son of 'Abdullah, the Messenger of Allah, may the peace and blessings of Allah be upon him, to all the Christians.

As sureties for the fulfillment of all that is prescribed herein, the following persons set theirs hands.

The names of the witnesses:

'Ali ibn Abi Talib; Abu Bakr ibn Abi Quhafah; 'Umar ibn al-Khatab; 'Uthman ibn 'Affan; Abu al-Darda'; Abi Hurayrah; 'Abd Allah ibn Ma'sud; 'Abbas ibn 'Abd al-Muttalib; Harith ibn Thabit; 'Abd al-'Azim ibn Hasan; Fudayl ibn 'Abbas; al-Zubayr ibn al-'Awwam; Talhah ibn 'Abd Allah; Sa'd ibn Mu'adh; Sa'd ibn 'Ubadah; Thabit ibn Nafis; Zayd ibn Thabit; Bu Hanifah ibn 'Ubayyah; Hashim ibn 'Ubayyah; Mu'azzam ibn Qurashi; 'Abd Allah ibn 'Amr ibn al-'As; 'Ammar ibn Yasir.

This covenant was written in his own hand by 'Ali ibn Abi Talib in the Mosque of the Prophet, may the peace and blessings of Allah be upon him, on the third of Muharram in the second year of the Prophet's Hegira.

A copy of this covenant has been deposited in the treasury of the Sultan. It was signed with the seal of the Prophet, peace be upon him. It was written on a piece of leather from Ta'if.

Blessed be he who abides by its contents. Blessed be he for he belongs to those who can expect the forgiveness of Allah.

This copy, which is copied from the original, is sealed with the signature of the noble Sultan. This reproduction was copied from the copy that was copied from the copy written in the handwriting of the Leader of the Believers, 'Ali ibn Abi Talib, may Allah bless his countenance.

With the order of the noble Sultan, that is still in effect, with the help of Allah, which was given to a community of monks who inhabit the Mountain of Tur-i Sina because the copy, which was copied from the copy written by the Leader of the Believers, was lost, in order that his document be a support of the Sultan's royal decrees which are evidenced by the records in the hands of the community in question.

This is a reproduction of the original without adaptation.

Written by the weakest of slaves,
al-Bari Nuh ibn Ahmad al-Ansari
The judge from Egypt, the Safeguarded, has pardoned them.
Sealed with the round seal and certified.
Nuh Ahmad ibn al-Ansari
[signature]
Modeled on a seal whose original is signed with this signature.
Written by the poor, Muhammad al-Qadi, from Ancient Egypt, may he be forgiven!

(Morrow 2015: 13-16).

Appendix 4 – The Treaty of Peace and Friendship

The following text was produced by the Avalon Project, which is based at the Lillian Goldman Law Library at Yale Law School.

Treaty of Peace and Friendship, signed at Tripoli November 4, 1796 (3 Ramada I, A. H. 1211), and at Algiers January 3, 1797 (4 Rajab, A. H. 1211). Original in Arabic. Submitted to the Senate May 29, 1797. (Message of May 26, 1797.) Resolution of advice and consent June 7, 1797. Ratified by the United States June 10, 1797. As to the ratification generally, see the notes. Proclaimed Jane 10, 1797.

The following fourteen pages of Arabic are a reproduction of the text in the original treaty book, first the pages of the treaty in left-to-right order of pagination, and then the " receipt " and the " note " mentioned, according to the Barlow translation, in Article 10. Following the Arabic and in the same order, is the translation of Joel Barlow as written in the treaty book-the twelve articles of the treaty, the "receipt," and the "note"; and after these is the approval of David Humphreys from the same document, which is fully described in the notes. Following those texts is the annotated translation of 1930.

[Translation]

Treaty of Peace and Friendship between the United States of America and the Bey and Subjects of Tripoli of Barbary.

ARTICLE 1.

There is a firm and perpetual Peace and friendship between the United States of America and the Bey and subjects of Tripoli of Barbary, made by the free consent of both parties, and guaranteed by the most potent Dey & regency of Algiers.

ARTICLE 2.

If any goods belonging to any nation with which either of the parties is at war shall be loaded on board of vessels belonging to the other party they shall pass free, and no attempt shall be made to take or detain them.

ARTICLE 3.

If any citizens, subjects or effects belonging to either party shall be found on board a prize vessel taken from an enemy by the other party, such citizens or subjects shall be set at liberty, and the effects restored to the owners.

ARTICLE 4.

Proper passports are to be given to all vessels of both parties, by which they are to be known. And, considering the distance between the two countries, eighteen months from the date of this treaty shall be allowed for procuring such passports. During this interval the other papers belonging to such vessels shall be sufficient for their protection.

ARTICLE 5.

A citizen or subject of either party having bought a prize vessel condemned by the other party or by any other nation, the certificate of condemnation and bill of sale shall be a sufficient passport for such vessel for one year; this being a reasonable time for her to procure a proper passport.

ARTICLE 6.

Vessels of either party putting into the ports of the other and having need of provissions or other supplies, they shall be furnished at the market price. And if any such vessel shall so put in from a disaster at sea and have occasion to repair, she shall be at liberty to land and reembark her cargo without paying any duties. But in no case shall she be compelled to land her cargo.

ARTICLE 7.

Should a vessel of either party be cast on the shore of the other, all proper assistance shall be given to her and her people; no pillage shall be allowed; the property shall remain at the disposition of the owners, and the crew protected and succoured till they can be sent to their country.

ARTICLE 8.

If a vessel of either party should be attacked by an enemy within gun-shot of the forts of the other she shall be defended as much as possible. If she be in port she shall not be seized or attacked when it is in the power of the other party to protect her. And when she proceeds to sea no enemy shall be allowed to pursue her from the same port within twenty four hours after her departure.

ARTICLE 9.

The commerce between the United States and Tripoli,-the protection to be given to merchants, masters of vessels and seamen,- the reciprocal right of establishing consuls in each country, and the privileges, immunities and jurisdictions to be enjoyed by such consuls, are declared to be on the same footing with those of the most favoured nations respectively.

ARTICLE 10.

The money and presents demanded by the Bey of Tripoli as a full and satisfactory consideration on his part and on the part of his subjects for this treaty of perpetual peace and friendship are acknowledged to have been recieved by him previous to his signing the same, according to a reciept which is hereto annexed, except such part as is promised on the part of the United States to be delivered and paid by them on the arrival of their Consul in Tripoly, of which part a note is likewise hereto annexed. And no presence of any periodical tribute or farther payment is ever to be made by either party.

ARTICLE 11.

As the government of the United States of America is not in any sense founded on the Christian Religion,-as it has in itself no character of enmity against the laws, religion or tranquility of Musselmen,-and as the said States never have entered into any war or act of hostility against any Mehomitan nation, it is declared by the parties that no pretext arising from religious opinions shall ever produce an interruption of the harmony existing between the two countries.

ARTICLE 12.

In case of any dispute arising from a notation of any of the articles of this treaty no appeal shall be made to arms, nor shall war be declared on any pretext whatever. But if the (consul residing at the place where the dispute shall happen shall not be able to settle the same, an amicable referrence shall be made to the mutual friend of the parties, the Dey of Algiers, the parties hereby engaging to abide by his decision. And he by virtue of his signature to this treaty engages for himself and successors to declare the justice of the case according to the true interpretation of the treaty, and to use all the means in his power to enforce the observance of the same.

Signed and sealed at Tripoli of Barbary the 3d day of Jumad in the year of the Higera 1211-corresponding with the 4th day of Novr 1796 by
JUSSUF BASHAW MAHOMET Bey
SOLIMA Kaya
MAMET Treasurer
GALIL Genl of the Troops
AMET Minister of Marine
MAHOMET Coml of the city
AMET Chamberlain
MAMET Secretary
ALLY – Chief of the Divan
Signed and sealed at Algiers the 4th day of Argib 1211 – corresponding with the 3d day of January 1797 by
HASSAN BASHAW Dey
And by the Agent plenipotentiary of the United States of America
[Seal] Joel BARLOW

Appendix 5

The following text is officially titled "A Document on Human Fraternity for World Peace and Living Together. It was agreed to by His Holiness Pope Francis and the Grand Imam of Al-Azhar, Ahmad Al-Tayyeb, on Pope Francis apostolic journey to the United Arab Emirates between February 3rd and February 5th of 2019. The text reads as follows:

Introduction

Faith leads a believer to see in the other a brother or sister to be supported and loved. Through faith in God, who has created the universe, creatures and all human beings (equal on account of his mercy), believers are called to express this human fraternity by safeguarding creation and the entire universe and supporting all persons, especially the poorest and those most in need.

This transcendental value served as the starting point for several meetings characterized by a friendly and fraternal atmosphere where we shared the joys, sorrows and problems of our contemporary world. We did this by considering scientific and technical progress, therapeutic achievements, the digital era, the mass media and communications. We reflected also on the level of poverty, conflict and suffering of so many brothers and sisters in different parts of the world as a consequence of the arms race, social injustice, corruption, inequality, moral decline, terrorism, discrimination, extremism and many other causes.

From our fraternal and open discussions, and from the meeting that expressed profound hope in a bright future for all human beings, the idea of this Document on *Human Fraternity* was conceived. It is a text that has been given honest and serious thought so as to be a joint declaration of good and heartfelt aspirations. It is a document that invites all persons who have faith in God and faith in *human fraternity* to unite and work together so that it may serve as a guide for future generations to advance a culture of mutual respect in the awareness of the great divine grace that makes all human beings brothers and sisters.

Document

In the name of God who has created all human beings equal in rights, duties and dignity, and who has called them to live together as brothers and sisters, to fill the earth and make known the values of goodness, love and peace;

In the name of innocent human life that God has forbidden to kill, affirming that whoever kills a person is like one who kills the whole of humanity, and that whoever saves a person is like one who saves the whole of humanity;

In the name of the poor, the destitute, the marginalized and those most in need whom God has commanded us to help as a duty required of all persons, especially the wealthy and of means;

In the name of orphans, widows, refugees and those exiled from their homes and their countries; in the name of all victims of wars, persecution and injustice; in the name of the weak, those who live in fear, prisoners of war and those tortured in any part of the world, without distinction;

In the name of peoples who have lost their security, peace, and the possibility of living together, becoming victims of destruction, calamity and war;

In the name of *human fraternity* that embraces all human beings, unites them and renders them equal;

In the name of this *fraternity* torn apart by policies of extremism and division, by systems of unrestrained profit or by hateful ideological tendencies that manipulate the actions and the future of men and women;

In the name of freedom, that God has given to all human beings creating them free and distinguishing them by this gift;

In the name of justice and mercy, the foundations of prosperity and the cornerstone of faith;

In the name of all persons of good will present in every part of the world;

In the name of God and of everything stated thus far; Al-Azhar al-Sharif and the Muslims of the East and West, together with the Catholic Church and the Catholics of the East and West, declare the adoption of a culture of dialogue as the path; mutual cooperation as the code of conduct; reciprocal understanding as the method and standard.

We, who believe in God and in the final meeting with Him and His judgment, on the basis of our religious and moral responsibility, and through this Document, call upon ourselves, upon the leaders of the world as well as the architects of international policy and world economy, to work strenuously to spread the culture of tolerance and of living together in peace; to intervene at the earliest opportunity to stop the shedding of innocent blood and bring an end to wars, conflicts, environmental decay and the moral and cultural decline that the world is presently experiencing.

We call upon intellectuals, philosophers, religious figures, artists, media professionals and men and women of culture in every part of the world, to rediscover the values of peace, justice, goodness, beauty, human fraternity and coexistence in order to confirm the importance of these values as anchors of salvation for all, and to promote them everywhere.

This Declaration, setting out from a profound consideration of our contemporary reality, valuing its successes and in solidarity with its suffering, disasters and calamities, believes firmly that among the most important causes of the crises of the modern world are a desensitized human conscience, a distancing from religious values and a prevailing individualism accompanied by materialistic philosophies that deify the human person and introduce worldly and material values in place of supreme and transcendental principles.

While recognizing the positive steps taken by our modern civilization in the fields of science, technology, medicine, industry and welfare, especially in developed countries, we wish to emphasize that, associated with such historic advancements, great and valued as they are, there exists both a moral deterioration that influences international action and a weakening of spiritual values and responsibility. All this contributes to a general feeling of frustration, isolation and desperation leading many to fall either into a vortex of atheistic, agnostic or religious extremism, or into blind and fanatic extremism, which ultimately encourage forms of dependency and individual or collective self-destruction.

History shows that religious extremism, national extremism and also intolerance have produced in the world, be it in the East or West, what might be referred to as signs of a "third world war being fought piecemeal". In several parts of the world and in many tragic circumstances these signs have begun to be painfully apparent, as in those situations where the precise number of victims, widows and orphans is unknown. We see, in addition, other regions preparing to become theatres of new conflicts, with outbreaks of tension and a build-up of arms and ammunition, and all this in a global context overshadowed by uncertainty, disillusionment, fear of the future, and controlled by narrow-minded economic interests.

We likewise affirm that major political crises, situations of injustice and lack of equitable distribution of natural resources – which only a rich minority benefit from, to the detriment of the majority of the peoples of the earth – have generated, and continue to generate, vast numbers of poor, infirm and deceased persons. This leads to catastrophic crises that various countries have fallen victim to despite their natural resources and the resourcefulness of young people which characterize these nations. In the face of such crises that result in the deaths of millions of children – wasted away from poverty and hunger – there is an unacceptable silence on the international level.

It is clear in this context how the family as the fundamental nucleus of society and humanity is essential in bringing children into the world, raising them, educating them, and providing them with solid moral formation and domestic security. To attack the institution of the family, to regard it with contempt or to doubt its important role, is one of the most threatening evils of our era.

We affirm also the importance of awakening religious awareness and the need to revive this awareness in the hearts of new generations through sound education and an adherence to moral values and upright religious teachings. In this way we can confront tendencies that are individualistic, selfish, conflicting, and also address radicalism and blind extremism in all its forms and expressions.

The first and most important aim of religions is to believe in God, to honour Him and to invite all men and women to believe that this universe depends on a God who governs it. He is the Creator who has formed us with His divine wisdom and has granted us the gift of life to protect it. It is a gift that no one has the right to take away, threaten or manipulate to suit oneself. Indeed, everyone must safeguard this gift of life from its beginning up to its natural end. We therefore condemn all those practices that are a threat to life such as genocide, acts of terrorism, forced displacement, human organ trafficking, abortion and euthanasia. We likewise condemn the policies that promote these practices.

Moreover, we resolutely declare that religions must never incite war, hateful attitudes, hostility and extremism, nor must they incite violence or the shedding of blood. These tragic realities are the consequence of a deviation from religious teachings. They result from a political manipulation of religions and from interpretations made by religious groups who, in the course of history, have taken advantage of the power of religious sentiment in the hearts of men and women in order to make them act in a way that has nothing to do with the truth of religion. This is done for the purpose of achieving objectives that are political, economic, worldly and short-sighted. We thus call upon all concerned to stop using religions to incite hatred, violence, extremism and blind fanaticism, and to refrain from using the name of God to justify acts of murder, exile, terrorism and oppression. We ask this on the basis of our common belief in God who did not create men and women to be killed or to fight one another, nor to be tortured or humiliated in their lives and circumstances. God, the Almighty, has no need to be defended by anyone and does not want His name to be used to terrorize people.

This Document, in accordance with previous International Documents that have emphasized the importance of the role of religions in the construction of world peace, upholds the following:

- The firm conviction that authentic teachings of religions invite us to remain rooted in the values of peace; to defend the values of mutual understanding, *human fraternity* and harmonious coexistence; to re-establish wisdom, justice and love; and to reawaken religious awareness among young people so that future generations may be protected from the realm of materialistic thinking and from dangerous policies of unbridled greed and indifference that are based on the law of force and not on the force of law;

- Freedom is a right of every person: each individual enjoys the freedom of belief, thought, expression and action. The pluralism and the diversity of religions, colour, sex, race and language are willed by God in His wisdom, through which He created human beings. This divine wisdom is the source from which the right to freedom of belief and the freedom to be different derives. Therefore, the fact that people are forced to adhere to a certain religion or culture must be rejected, as too the imposition of a cultural way of life that others do not accept;

- Justice based on mercy is the path to follow in order to achieve a dignified life to which every human being has a right;

- Dialogue, understanding and the widespread promotion of a culture of tolerance, acceptance of others and of living together peacefully would contribute significantly to reducing many economic, social, political and environmental problems that weigh so heavily on a large part of humanity;

- Dialogue among believers means coming together in the vast space of spiritual, human and shared social values and, from here, transmitting the highest moral virtues that religions aim for. It also means avoiding unproductive discussions;

- The protection of places of worship – synagogues, churches and mosques – is a duty guaranteed by religions, human values, laws and international agreements. Every attempt to attack places of worship or threaten them by violent assaults, bombings or destruction, is a deviation from the teachings of religions as well as a clear violation of international law;

- Terrorism is deplorable and threatens the security of people, be they in the East or the West, the North or the South, and disseminates panic, terror and pessimism, but this is not due to religion, even when terrorists instrumentalize it. It is due, rather, to an accumulation of incorrect interpretations of religious texts and to policies linked to hunger, poverty, injustice, oppression and pride. This is why it is so necessary to stop supporting terrorist movements fueled by financing, the provision of weapons and strategy, and by attempts to justify these movements even using the media. All these must be regarded as international crimes that threaten security and world peace. Such terrorism must be condemned in all its forms and expressions;

- The concept of *citizenship* is based on the equality of rights and duties, under which all enjoy justice. It is therefore crucial to establish in our societies the concept of *full citizenship* and reject the discriminatory use of the term *minorities* which engenders feelings of isolation and inferiority. Its misuse paves the way for hostility and discord; it undoes any successes and takes away the religious and civil rights of some citizens who are thus discriminated against;

- Good relations between East and West are indisputably necessary for both. They must not be neglected, so that each can be enriched by the other's culture through fruitful exchange and dialogue. The West can discover in the East remedies for those spiritual and religious maladies that are caused by a prevailing materialism. And the East can find in the West many elements that can help free it from weakness, division, conflict and scientific, technical and cultural decline. It is important to pay attention to religious, cultural and historical differences that are a vital component in shaping the character, culture and civilization of the East. It is likewise important to reinforce the bond of fundamental human rights in order to help ensure a dignified life for all the men and women of East and West, avoiding the politics of double standards;

- It is an essential requirement to recognize the right of women to education and employment, and to recognize their freedom to exercise their own political rights. Moreover, efforts must be made to free women from historical and social conditioning that runs contrary to the principles of their faith and dignity. It is also necessary to protect women from sexual exploitation and from being treated as merchandise or objects of pleasure or financial gain. Accordingly, an end must be brought to all those inhuman and vulgar practices that denigrate the dignity of women. Efforts must be made to modify those laws that prevent women from fully enjoying their rights;

- The protection of the fundamental rights of children to grow up in a family environment, to receive nutrition, education and support, are duties of the family and society. Such duties must be guaranteed and protected so that they are not overlooked or denied to any child in any part of the world. All those practices that violate the dignity and rights of children must be denounced. It is equally important to be vigilant against the dangers that they are exposed to, particularly in the digital world, and to consider as a crime the trafficking of their innocence and all violations of their youth;

- The protection of the rights of the elderly, the weak, the disabled, and the oppressed is a religious and social obligation that must be guaranteed and defended through strict legislation and the implementation of the relevant international agreements.

To this end, by mutual cooperation, the Catholic Church and Al-Azhar announce and pledge to convey this Document to authorities, influential leaders, persons of religion all over the world, appropriate regional and international organizations, organizations within civil society, religious institutions and leading thinkers. They further pledge to make known the principles contained in this Declaration at all regional and international levels, while requesting that these principles be translated into policies, decisions, legislative texts, courses of study and materials to be circulated.

Al-Azhar and the Catholic Church ask that this Document become the object of research and reflection in all schools, universities and institutes of formation, thus helping to educate new generations to bring goodness and peace to others, and to be defenders everywhere of the rights of the oppressed and of the least of our brothers and sisters.

In conclusion, our aspiration is that:

this Declaration may constitute an invitation to reconciliation and fraternity among all believers, indeed among believers and non-believers, and among all people of good will;

this Declaration may be an appeal to every upright conscience that rejects deplorable violence and blind extremism; an appeal to those who cherish the values of tolerance and fraternity that are promoted and encouraged by religions;

this Declaration may be a witness to the greatness of faith in God that unites divided hearts and elevates the human soul;

this Declaration may be a sign of the closeness between East and West, between North and South, and between all who believe that God has created us to understand one another, cooperate with one another and live as brothers and sisters who love one another.

This is what we hope and seek to achieve with the aim of finding a universal peace that all can enjoy in this life.

Abu Dhabi, 4 February 2019

His Holiness Pope Francis

The Grand Imam of Al-Azhar, Ahmad Al-Tayyeb

Glossary

abayah – the Arabic word that refers to "cloak"; a simple, loose garment worn by Muslim women

ahl al-kitab – the Arabic term that refers to "People of the Book"; reference to the place of the Christian and Jewish faith within the Abrahamic tradition (monotheism)

al-Andalus – literally meaning "to become green at the end of the summer," al-Andalus is a medieval Muslim territory on the Iberian peninsula of Spain

al-Bukhari – Muslim scholar (d. 870) whose work (Sahih al-Bukhari) is one of the six canonical *Hadith* collections, or traditions of the Prophet *'aleem* – the Arabic term that refers to "knowledgeable man" or "learned man"

Allah – the Arabic word for God, as linked to the monotheistic tradition

as-salamalaikum – the Arabic phrase and Islamic concept that refers to the Muslim greeting that means "peace be upon you;" a standard salutation among Muslims

bismillah al-rahman al-rahim - the Arabic phrase and Islamic concept that refers to "In the Name of God, the Merciful, the Compassionate"

burqa –the Arabic word that refers to a long, loose article of clothing that covers the whole body from head to feet; worn in public by Muslim women

caliph – the Arabic word and Islamic concept that refers to the supreme Muslim head of state who governs over the political, social, religious, and cultural affairs of the global Muslim nation, or *ummah*

dhimmi – the Arabic word and Islamic concept that refers to members of other faith groups living in Muslim lands; also translated to mean "protected person"

emir – the Arabic word and Islamic concept that refers to a title of a Muslim ruler or commander of a "Muslim nation"

hajj – the Arabic word and Islamic concept that refers to the annual pilgrimage to Mecca required of all Muslims at least once in their lifetime (if they can afford it)

hadith (or Hadith)– the Arabic word and Islamic text that refers to a narrative report of Prophet Muhammad's sayings and actions *hijab* – the Arabic word which translates roughly to "veil," that also refers to something that conceals, covers, or protects against penetration between two things.

hijrah – the Arabic word that refers to "migration." The first *hijrah* in Islamic history occurred around 615 when the early Muslim community sought asylum in the Christian kingdom of Abyssinia

ilm – the Arabic word that refers to "knowledge"

iqra – an Arabic word that refers to "read"

jabal – the Arabic word that refers to "mountain"

jahiliyyah – the Arabic word and Islamic concept that refers to "ignorance of divine guidance;" refers to the period of Arabia before God's revelations to Prophet Muhammad

jihad – the Arabic word and Islamic concept that refers to "striving"; refers specifically to the effort or struggle involved in following Islam so as to excel in faith; can include physical defense of the faith

jizya – the Arabic word and Islamic concept that refers to a per capita yearly tax historically levied by Islamic governments on non-Muslims, or *dhimmi* ("protected person")

kumabaya – the Gullah (a branch of the Creole language) term that refers to "come by here"

la Convivencia – the Spanish phrase that refers to "coexistence;" also, an academic hypothesis regarding the period of history (711 to 1492) in which Muslims ruled Spain

masjid – the Arabic word that refers to mosque

millet – the Turkish term that refers to an independent court and legal system of the Ottoman Empire that allowed religious minority populations to rule themselves according to their religious laws

muezzin – the Arabic word that refers to a man who calls Muslims to prayer from the tower of a mosque

mufti – the Arabic terms that refers to a learned Muslim who serves as a preeminent leader on matters of Islamic theology and jurisprudence

Muqaddimah – the book written by Arab historian Ibn Khaldun in 1377; records a view of early history

qadi – the Arabic word that refers to "magistrate" or "judge" in an Islamic law court *qantara* – the Arabic word that refers to "bridge"

Qur'an – the Arabic word that refers to the holy book of Islam

seerah – the Arabic term that refers to the study of the life of Prophet Muhammad and other matters relating to him

shahada – the Arabic term and Islamic concept that refers to the "Islamic testament of faith," which reads: "There is no God but God, and Muhammad is the messenger of God"

sharia – the Arabic word that refers to the "path" or "the path to the watering hole"; also known as "Islamic law"

Stupor Mondi – the Latin word that refers to "astonishment of the world;" used in light of the legacy of Frederick II, former Holy Roman Emperor

Sunnah – the Arabic term that refers to traditional Islamic customs and practices, in the social and legal realms, that Muslims are commanded to follow as prescribed by Muhammad

suq al-'attarin – the Arabic phrase that refers to "market of the perfumers"

tawhid – the Arabic word and Islamic concept that refers to "oneness" of God

ujb – the Arabic word that refers to "pride" or "arrogance"

ummah – the Arabic term and Islamic concept that refers to "Islamic community," refers to the worldwide Muslim population

BIBLIOGRAPHY

60 Minutes. n.d. "The Holy Prophet Muhammad's Letter to the Monks of St. Catherine in Mt. Sinai." YouTube. Retrieved online https://www.youtube.com/watch?v=u0SsRmC6O5k

Allen Jr. John L. 2013. "Francis and the 'Culture of Encounter.'" National Catholic Reporter, December 20. Retrieved online https://www.ncronline.org/blogs/ncr-today/francis-and-culture-encounter

Armstrong, Karen. 2000. *Islam: A Short History*. New York: Modern Library.

———. 2006. *Muhammad: A Prophet of Our Time*. New York: Harper Collins.

Arocho Esteves, Junno. 2019. "Pope Francis: Religious fundamentalism is a 'plague.'" America Magazine, November 19. Retrieved online https://www.americamagazine.org/faith/2019/11/19/pope-francis-religious-fundamentalism-plague

———. 2019. "Pope: Respect, dialogue key for peace between Christians, Muslims." National Catholic Reporter, February 6. Retrieved online https://www.ncronline.org/news/vatican/francis-chronicles/pope-respect-dialogue-key-peace-between-christians-muslims

Asaad, Fakir Muhammad Asaad. 2009. *Practical Philosophy Of The Muhammadan People: Being a Translation of the Akhlak-i-Jalaly* (1839). Whitefish, MT: Kessinger Publishing.

Avnery. 2004. "Identifying the Virus – Who is Antisemitic and Who is Not?" *New York Times*, January 28. Retrieved online https://www.nytimes.com/2004/01/28/opinion/identifying-the-virus-who-is-antisemitic-and-who-is-not.html

Baldock, John. 2006. *The Essence of Rumi*. London: Acturus.

Baraz, Yevgeniya. 2010. "The Position of Jews and Christians in the Ottoman Empire." *Inquiries* 2(5): 1.

Barkey, Karen and George Gavrilis. 2015. "The Ottoman Millet System: Non-Territorial Autonomy and its Contemporary Legacy." *Ethnopolitics* 15(1): 24-42.

Barry, Brian. *Culture and Equality*. Cambridge, MA: Harvard University Press.

Blumberg, Antonia. 2017. "Who Are Egypt's Coptic Christians and What Do They Believe?" Huffington Post, April 10. Retrieved online https://www.huffpost.com/entry/who-are-egypts-coptic-christians-and-what-do-they-believe_n_58ebc537e4b0c89f912058d5

Boase, Roger. 1990. "The Morisco Expulsion and Diaspora: An Example of Racial and Religious Intolerance" in David Hook, Barry Taylor, and Leonard Patrick Harvey (Eds) *Culture in Contact in Medieval Spain: Historical and Literary Essays Presented to L.P. Harvey*. London: Kings College, Medieval Studies.

Chaudhry, Kashif N. 2016. "Did Prophet Muhammad Warn Us of ISIS? Huff Post, June 30th. Retrieved online https://www.huffpost.com/entry/did-prophet-mu-hammad-warn_b_7702064.

Cole, Juan. 2018. *Muhammad: Prophet of Peace Amid the Clash of Empires*. New York: Nation Books.

Considine, Craig. 2013. "A New Perspective of 'Jihad' in Christianity and Islam." Huff Post, October 5. Retrieved online from https://www.huffpost.com/entry/a-new-perspective-of-jiha_b_3650433.

——. 2013. "An Unlikely Connection Between the Prophet Muhammad and George Washington." Huff Post, March 12. Retrieved online from https://www.huffpost.com/entry/an-unlikely-connection-between-the-prophet-mu-hammad-and-george-washington_b_2439940.

——. 2013. "Rumi and Emerson: A Bridge Between the West and the Muslim World." Huff Post, October 14. Retrieved online from https://www.huffpost.com/entry/rumi-and-emerson_b_3748667.

——. 2014. "Overcoming Historical Amnesia: Muslim Contributions to Civilization." Huff Post, January 23. Retrieved online from https://www.huffpost.com/entry/overcoming-historical-amnesia_b_4135868.

——. 2014. "The Problem With Banning the Burqa." Huff Post, May 12. Retrieved online from https://www.huffpost.com/entry/the-problem-with-banning-the-burqa_b_4940212.

——. 2015. "Jesus Christ and Prophet Muhammad Followed 'The Golden Rule.'" Huff Post, June 21. Retrieved online from https://www.huffpost.com/entry/je-sus-christ-and-prophet-_b_7110104.

——. 2016a. "Religious Pluralism and Civic Rights in a 'Muslim Nation': An Analy-sis of Prophet Muhammad's Covenants with Christians." *Religions* 7(15): 1-21.

——. 2016b. "Prophet Muhammad stood for humanity in Medina, while IS tries to destroy it." Middle East Eye. July 11. Retrieved online https://www.mid-dleeasteye.net/opinion/prophet-muhammad-stood-humanity-medi-na-while-tries-destroy-it.

——. 2016c. "Christians and Muslims Should Embrace 'The Jihad of Jesus.'" Huff Post, May 31. Retrieved online from https://www.huffpost.com/entry/chris-tians-and-muslims-sh_b_7480898.

——. 2017. "The Other Al-Andalus – When Muslims and Christians Flourished Side By Side in Sicily." Huff Post, April 22. Retrieved online from https://www.huffpost.com/entry/the-other-alandalus_b_9730774.

——. 2018. *Muslims in America: Examining the Facts*. Santa Barbara, CA: ABC-CLIO.

——. 2019. *Islam in America: Exploring the Issues*. Santa Barbara, CA: ABC-CLIO.

Dardess, George. 2005. *Meeting Islam: A Guide for Christians*. Brewster, Massachusetts: Paraclete Press.

Denny, Frederick M. 1977. "*Ummah* in the Constitution of Medina." *Journal of Near Eastern Studies* 36: 39-47.

Draper, John William. 1878. *History of the Conflict Between Religion and Science*. New York, NY: D. Appleton & Co.

Eck, Diana L. (2006). "What is Pluralism." The Pluralism Project – Harvard University. Retrieved online http://pluralism.org/what-is-pluralism/

Essa, Ahmed with Othman Ali. 2010. *Studies in Islamic Civilization: The Muslim Contribution to the Renaissance*. Herndon, Virginia: The International Institute of Islamic Thought.

Eviv, Efrat. 2016. "Millet System in the Ottoman Empire." Oxford Bibliographies. Retrieved online https://www.oxfordbibliographies.com/view/document/obo-9780195390155/obo-9780195390155-0231.xml

Faryab, Mohamamd Hossein Faryab. 2012. "The Status of Knowledge in Islam." *Message of Thaqalayn* 13(1): 73-100.

Feiler, Bruce. 2002. *Abraham: A Journey to the Heart of Three Faiths*. New York: Harper Collins.

Franklin, Benjamin. 1856. *The Works of Benjamin Franklin; Containing Several Political and Historical Tracts Not Included in Any Former Edition and Many Letters Official and Private, Not Hitherto Published; with Notes and a Life of the Author*, edited by Jared Sparks. Boston, Massachusetts: Whittemore, Niles, and Hall.

———. 1986. *Benjamin Franklin's Autobiography*, edited by J.A. Leo LeMay and P.M. Zail. New York: W.W. Norton & Co. 87-88.

Gil, Moshe. 1974. "The Constitution of Medina: A Reconsideration." *Israel Oriental Studies* 4: 44-66.

Gryboski, Michael. 2019. "Christians risk arrest if they display Bible in Saudi Arabia, persecution watchdog group warns." Christian Post, October 16. Retrieved online https://www.christianpost.com/news/christians-risk-arrest-if-they-display-bible-in-saudi-arabia-persecution-watchdog-group-warns.html

Guillaume, Alfred. 2017. *The Life of Muhammad: A Translation of Ibn Ishaq's Sirat Rasul Allah*. Karachi: Oxford University Press. Thirst-first impression. p. 53.

Gülen, M. Fethullah. 2016. *The Messenger of God Muhammad: An Analysis of the Prophet's Life*. Somerset, New Jersey: The Light.

Hadro, Matt. 2019. "South and East Asia now the hotbed of Christian persecution, report finds." Catholic News Agency. Retrieved online https://www.catholicnewsagency.com/news/south-and-east-asia-now-the-hotbed-of-christian-persecution-report-finds-92385

Hamidullah, Muhammad. 1975. *The First Written Constitution of the World: An Important Document of the Time of the Holy Prophet*. Lahore: Sh. Muhammad Ashraf.

———. 1998. *The Life and Work of the Prophet of Islam*. Translated in English and Edited by Mahmood Ahmed Ghazi. India: Adam Publishers. p. 279.

Hart, Michael H. 1978. *The 100: A Ranking of the Most Influential Persons in History*. New York, New York: Citadel Press.

Huntington, Samuel. 2011. *The Clash of Civilizations and the Remaking of World Order*. New York: Simon and Schuster.

Ibrahim, Azeem. 2019. "ISIS's Church Attacks Break Mohammed's Own Pledges." For-

eign Policy, May 8. Retrieved online https://foreignpolicy.com/2019/05/08/
isiss-church-attacks-break-mohammeds-own-pledges/

Ignatieff, Michael. (1993). *Blood and Belonging: Journeys into the New Nationalism*. New
York, NY: Farrar, Straus, and Giroux.

Irving, Washington. 1855. *The Life of Mahomet*. London: Henry G. Bohn.

Kaskas, Safi and David Hungerford. 2016. *The Qur'an With References to the Bible*. Fair-
fax, Virginia: Bridges of Reconciliation.

Kayaoglu, Turan. 2012. "Constructing the dialogue of civilizations in world politics: a
case of global Islamic activism." *Islam and Christian-Muslim Relations* 23,
no. 2: 129-47.

Kennedy, Hugh. n.d. "Was Islam Spread by the Sword?" The MacMillan Center: Yale
University. Retrieved from https://rps.macmillan.yale.edu/sites/default/
files/files/kennedy.pdf

Kenny, Allyson. 2019. "The Sultan and the Saint." Salt and Light Media, February 4. Retrieved online https://saltandlighttv.org/blogfeed/getpost.
php?id=89164

Khan, Maulana Wahiduddin. 2016. *Muhammad: A Prophet for All Humanity*. India:
Goodword Books.

Khatami, Mohammad. 2001. *Dialogue among Civilizations: The Round Table on the Eve
of the United nations Milennium Summit*. Paris, France, UNESCO. Retrieved
online http://unescodoc.unesco.org/images/0012/001238/123890E.pdf

Khoury, Jack. 2017. "Egypt: ISIS Gunmen Attack St. Catherine's Monastery in Sinai."
Haaretz, April 19. Retrieved online https://www.haaretz.com/middle-
east-news/egypt/egypt-isis-gunmen-attack-st-catherine-s-monastery-in-
sinai-1.5462205

King, Lagarrett. 2016. "Black History as Anti-Racist and Non-Racist: An Examination of
Two High School Black History Textbooks." In *But I Don't See Color: The
Perils, Practices, and Possibilities of Antiracist Education* by Terry Husband
(editor). Rotterdam: Sense Publishers.

Lapidus, Ira M. 1975. "The Separation of State and Religion in the Development of Early
Islamic Society." *International Journal of Middle East Studies* 6: 364.

Lewis, Bernard. 2003. *What Went Wrong? The Clash Between Islam and Modernity in the
Middle East*. New York: Harper Collins.

Lings, Martin. 2006. *Muhammad: His Life Based on the Earliest Sources*. Rochester, Ver-
mont: Inner Traditions.

Morrow, John Andrew. 2013. *The Covenants of the Prophet Muhammad with the Christians of the World*. Tacoma, WA: Angelico Press/Sophia Perennis.

——— (editor). 2015. *Six Covenants of the Prophet Muhammad with the Christians of His
Time: The Primary Documents*. Tacoma: Covenants Press.

——— (editor). 2017. *Islam and the People of the Book: Critical Studies of the Covenants of the
Prophet (Vol. 1-3)*. Newcastle upon Tyne: Cambridge Scholars Publishing.

Naji, Ma'rouf. 1968. Thaqafat Al-Baghdadiyin (The Baghdadies Culture). In *Baghdad: An
Illustrated Historical Exposition* by Mustafa Jawad, Ahmad Susa, Mohammad Makiya, and Ma'rouf Naji. Baghdad: Iraqi Society of Engineers.

Owolawi, Wahab. 2017. *Dialogue With the Self: Unlocking the Door to Your True Self.* Ishpeming, MI: Book Venture.

Oxford Islamic Studies Online. (n.d.). "Asabiyya." The Oxford Dictionary of Islam. Retrieved online http://www.oxfordislamicstudies.com/article/opr/t125/e202

Pope Francis. 2016. "For a culture of encounter." *L'Osservatore Romano*, September 23. Retrieved online https://w2.vatican.va/content/francesco/en/cotidie/2016/documents/papa-francesco-cotidie_20160913_for-a-culture-of-encounter.html

Rao, K.S. Ramakrishna. 1978. *Mohammad: The Prophet of Islam.* World Assembly of Muslim Youth, 86(2): 1-36.

Rashid, Qasim. 2017. "Muslim men need to understand that the Quran says they should observe hijab first, not women." The Independent, March 29. Retrieved online https://www.independent.co.uk/voices/muslim-men-hijab-forcing-women-islam-teaching-mohammed-quran-modesty-a7655191.html

Ruiz, Rebecca. 2019. "6 ways to be antiracist, because being 'not racist' isn't enough." Mashable, August 13. Retrieved online https://mashable.com/article/how-to-be-antiracist/

Scarfiotti, Gian Luigi and Lunde, Paul. 1978. "Muslim Sicily." *Aramco World*, November/December. Retrieved online from https://archive.aramcoworld.com/issue/197806/muslim.sicily.htm

Scott, Samuel Parsons Scott. 1904. *History of the Moorish Empire in Europe.* Philadelphia & London: J.B. Lippincott Company.

Sedarat, Roger. 2019. *Emerson in Iran: The American Appropriation of Persian Poetry.* Albany, NY: SUNY Press.

Shah, Niaz A. 2013. "The Use of Force under Islamic Law." *European Journal of International Law* 24(1): 343-364.

Shah-Kazemi, Reza. 2012. *The Spirit of Tolerance in Islam.* London & New York: I.B. Tauris.

Siddiqui, Mona. 2013. *Christians, Muslims, and Jesus.* New Haven and London: Yale University Press.

Stilz, Anna. (2009). "Civic Nationalism and Language Policy." *Philosophy & Public Affairs*, 37: 257-292.

Taylor, Ericka. 2019. "Ibram X. Kendi Aays No One Is 'Not Racist.' So What Should We Do?" National Public Radio, August 15. Retrieved online https://www.npr.org/2019/08/15/751070344/theres-no-such-thing-as-not-racist-in-ibram-x-kendis-how-to-be-an-anitracist

Wani, Zahid Ashraf and Maqbol, Tabasum. 2012. "The Islamic era and its importance to knowledge and the development of libraries." *Library Philosophy and Practice.* 1-4. Retrieved online https://digitalcommons.unl.edu/libphilprac/718/

Watt, W. Montgomery. 1953. *Muhammad at Mecca.* Oxford: Clarendon Press.

Yaqeen Institute for Islamic Research. 2017. "The Hadith and the Myth of an Antisemitic Genocide In Muslim Scripture." Huffington Post. March 28. Retrieved online https://www.huffpost.com/entry/the-jew-killing-hadith-and-the-myth-of-an-antisemitic_b_58da7e56e4b0e96354656eb6

NOTES

1   A *hadith* is a report of words, actions, or silent approvals of the Prophet Muhammad that were orally transmitted and then documented based on well recorded chains of transmission. These reports "can be incredibly complex as one needs to evaluate all the chains of transmission of a particular statement recorded in a *hadith* in order to arrive at an appropriate conclusion of what the particular *hadith* is actually talking about" (Yaqeen Institute for Islamic Research 2017).

2   This claim was made by Akbar Ahmed in the BBC online article titled "The pen, the sword and the prophet."

3   The verses of the Holy Qur'an cited in this book are provided by the website mquran.org.

4   The Holy Bible passages used in this book were retrieved from the *Good News Bible (With Deuterocanicals/Apocrypha) – Today's English Version (Second Edition)*. This translation of the Bible was published by William H. Sadlier, Inc. of New York in 1993.

5   A November 18th, 2016 *Washington Post* article by Thomas Gibbons-Neff reported a tweet by U.S. Army Lieutenant General Michael Flynn, who stated the following on Twitter: "Fear of Muslims is RATIONAL: please forward this to others: the truth fears no questions ..." Flynn included a link to a YouTube video which claimed that "Islamophobia is an oxymoron ... Fearing Islam, which wants 80 percent of humanity enslaved or exterminated, is totally rational, and hence cannot be considered a phobia." Flynn also briefly served as the National Security Advisor to President Donald Trump.

6   The Greek philosopher Socrates, who lived approximately from 470 BC to 399 BC, is one of the most important thinkers in terms of the development of Western philosophy, and indeed of philosophy at large. Socrates was a controversial and enigmatic figure in Ancient Athens because of his societal views and approach towards learning. Two of his students, Plato and Xenophon, portrayed him in their works as a man with great wisdom, integrity, and argumentative skill. Plato's *Apology of Socrates* is a report of the speech that Socrates gave at his

trial, during which he was accused of polluting the minds of the Athenian youth and threatening Athenian democracy.

7   Open Doors USA is a non-denominational 501c3, non-profit organization focused on supporting persecuted Christians in more than 70 countries across the world. The organization provides practical support, such as giving emergency relief aid, raising awareness on the persecution of Christians, distributing Christian literature, and offering training to emerging Christian leaders.

8   This excerpt was taken from the Pakistan country profile on the Open Doors USA website https://www.opendoorsusa.org/christian-persecution/world-watch-list/pakistan/

9   The Qur'anic term *ahl al kitab* is sometimes applied to Zoroastrians, Magians, and Samaritans as well, as noted by Oxford Islamic Studies (online).

10   The term *dhimmi*, as Considine (2019: 47) explains, is "an Arabic term relating to the treatment of religious minority populations living in a Muslim-majority society or under what may be called an 'Islamic state.'" The term translates to "non-Muslims living under the protection of the *sharia*, or Islamic law." Anti-Islam critics and polemicists claim that *dhimmi* is a permanent, oppressive status in which Jews, Christians, and groups of various faiths are forced to accept an unjust tax or face conversion, slavery, or death. Additional critics use the term "*dhimmi*tude" in alleging that groups like Jews and Christians are forced to appease and surrender to the *sharia* in Muslim-majority countries, and when describing the parlous state of religious minority populations who refuse to convert to the Islamic faith.

11   "Muslim Spain" or Al-Andalus is the name given to the period of history in which Muslims ruled over the Iberian Peninsula. The period is generally recognized as beginning in 711 and ending in 1492 with the "Christian Reconquista." The Iberian Peninsula during this period maintained a spirit of "*la Convivencia*," a Spanish term that means "living in togetherness" or "coexistence." This period in Islamic history, popularly referred to as Al-Andalus, is widely recognized as one that had an unprecedented level of interreligious engagement between Muslims, Christians, and Jews.

12   According to dictionary.com, *kumbaya* refers, often disparagingly, to moments of or efforts at harmony and unity. Although the origins of the term are disputed, *kumbaya* is linked to the African American traditions coming out of the Gullah culture of the islands of South Carolina and Georgia with ties to enslaved West Africans.

13   Tabari said that Abdullah ibn Abi Bakr, a companion of Prophet Muhammad and the son of Abu Bakr (the first caliph), was the narrator of Khalid ibn al-Walid's expedition to the city of Najran. See. Tabari, Abu Ja'far Muhammad bin Jarir. *The History of al-Tabari: The Last Years of the Prophet – The Formation of the State* A.D. 630-632/A.H. 8-11. 1990. Translated by Ismail K. Poonawala. Albany: State University of New York Press. p. 82-84. Further, Muhammad Hamidullah, a scholar of *sharia* (Islamic law) and an academic author of over 250 books, considers Abu Bakr's letters to be authentic. See: Hamidullah, Muhammad. 1998. *The Life and Work of the Prophet of Islam.* Translated in English and Edited by Mahmood Ahmed Ghazi. India: Adam Publishers. p. 279.

14   Christology is the branch of Christian theology that deals with the nature of Jesus and the role that he performed on Earth. This branch examines Jesus' human nature and divine qualities and the relationship between these entities in terms of human salvation.

15   Saint Catherine's monastery, a Greek-Orthodox community built in the 6th century, is located in a remote desert and mountainous region in the southern part of the Sinai peninsula of Egypt. The monastery is a popular tourist site in the area of the Red Sea.

16   The Coptic Christians are one of the oldest Christian communities in the world. Copts, as they are popularly known, trace their founding to Saint Mark, an apostle, who founded the Coptic Church in the 1st century. The Coptic Church, which falls under the realm of "Christianity Orthodoxy," split away from the international Christian community in 451, due mainly to its view that Jesus had two natures – one human and one divine.

17   John Andrew Morrow believes that the original copy is held at the Topkapi Museum, but when he contacted their staff through diplomatic channels, he was informed that the museum did not have the original in its collection: they did, however, have the copy Feridun Bey made of the original in the 16th century. Morrow's colleague, however, insists that he saw the original with his own eyes. While Morrow has not seen it himself, he is well-aware that the Topkapi Museum has previously revealed that they had a copy issued by Sultan Selim in 1517 (Morrow 2017: 14).

18   Sheikh El-Tayeb is currently the Grand Imam of Al-Azhar University and mosque, the leading Sunni Islamic institution of higher learning in the world. Al-Azhar was founded in the 10th century.

19   The encounter between Francis and al-Kamil was made into a documentary – "The Sultan and the Saint" – which premiered in December 2017.

20   Salt and Light Television is a Canadian multi-lingual television channel owned by the non-profit Salt and Light Catholic Media Foundation. The channel broadcasts Catholic-based programming to Catholics around the world.

21   Hitti, Philip K. 1970. *History of the Arabs* (Revised Edition). New York: St. Martin's Press.

22   Lapidus, Ira M. 1975. "The Separation of State and Religion in the Development of Early Islamic Society." *International Journal of Middle East Studies* 6: 364.

23   This claim needs to be placed into context, especially in light of the fact that many of the U.S. Founding Fathers owned slaves. Critics rightly note that many men in this collection of early Americans failed to rise above their time and place by freeing slaves. My contention is that the Founding Fathers had a vision for a kind of nation that would one day fix the evil wrong of slavery in favor of a more just society.

24   The Fifteenth Amendment of the U.S. Constitution similarly "prohibits the denial of suffrage based on race, color, or previous condition of servitude," which again cements a vision based on civic principles rather than absolutist or ethnocentric worldviews. However, the Fifteenth Amendment was ratified decades later, in 1870.

25   In a similar manner Thomas Jefferson, the co-author of the Declaration of Independence, helped to pass legislation in the Virginia state legislature that read: "the Jew, the Gentile, the Christian, and the [Muslim], the [Hindu], and infidel of every denomination" are accepted as equal citizens of the United States of America.

26   These states included the present-day countries of Algeria, Morocco, and Tunisia.

27   The Alhambra palace and fortress is located in the Spanish city of Granada. Originally built in 899 on the site of a Roman fortress, the Alhambra was converted into a royal palace by Sultan Yusuf I in 1333. The Alhambra is a United Nations Educational, Scientific and Cultural Organization (UNESCO) World Heritage Site that has had a significant influence on cultural activities including music and poetry.

28   The term "Turk" in the American colonies during the 18th century was used interchangeably with other terms like "Mohammedan," "Moslem," "Arab," and "Saracen."

29 A *mufti* is a Muslim that is considered to be a legal expert. Serving in this role allows a *mufti* to give rulings on religious matters that are considered to be authoritative in light of the *sharia*.

30 See the article "Racial Equality 'Is Under Attack,' Experts Warn General Assembly, Urging States to Mark International Day by Stamping out Discrimination, Intolerance," on the United Nations website.

31 Bilal was also the treasurer of the Prophet, another honorable position within the early *ummah*.

32 See the website malcolmx.com for a thorough biography of Malcolm X.

33 Passages in this section were first outlined in my Huff Post article titled "Overcoming Historical Amnesia: Muslim Contributions to Civilization."

34 The Guinness Book of World Records considers al-Qarawiyyin to be the oldest continually operating higher-learning institution and oldest university in the world. See: https://www.guinnessworldrecords.com/world-records/oldest-university?fb_comment_id=884703521549256_923508941002047

35 This rumor was touched upon by the Manchester University Press blog post titled "Fatima al-Fihri: Founder of the world's first university." See: https://manchester-universitypress.co.uk/articles/fatima-al-fihri-founder-worlds-first-university/

36 The Muslim contribution to the Renaissance, as Ahmed Essa (2010: xiv) noted, has either been minimized or completely overlooked. The reality of the matter is that Muslims played a synthesizing, creative, and intermediary role between the ancient Roman-Greek civilization and the Renaissance in Europe. For a complete analysis on the progress made by Islamic civilization and Muslims' contribution to the Renaissance, see *Studies in Islamic Civilization: The Muslim Contribution to the Renaissance* by Ahmed Essa with Othman Ali.

37 The Abbasid caliphate overthrew the Umayyad caliphate in 750 to emerge as the second of the two great dynasties of the Islamic empire. Under Abbasid rule the center of power of the "Muslim world" moved eastward from Damascus to Baghdad and Samarra. In the 10th century, the Abbasid hold on the Islamic empire weakened as semi-autonomous local dynasties rose in Egypt and Iran. The Abbasid caliphate lasted until the invasion of the Mongols in 1258.

38 The Mamluk dynasty emerged in Egypt and Syria and lasted from 1250 to 1517. The term Mamluk is derived from the Arabic word meaning "slave" or "owned." The Mamluks were not native to Egypt and Syria, but were rather slave soldiers that served in Islamic armies starting in the Abbasid caliphate in the 9th century.

The Mamluk dynasty was overthrown by the Ottomans who emerged as the next Islamic dynasty.

39   The flourishing civilization emanating from al-Andalus ended when the Sultan of Granada, King Ferdinand, and Queen Isabella signed the Treaty of Granada in 1492. Also known as the Capitulation of Granada, the treaty forced the Emirate of Granada to forfeit its territories and fortresses to the Catholic monarchy of Spain.

40   Additionally, Ibn Khaldun, who some scholars consider to be the founder of the academic discipline of sociology, developed the concept of *asabiyya*, an Arabic term which translates to "social solidarity." *Asabiyya* emphasizes the importance of group consciousness, cohesiveness, and unity. It is neither necessarily nomadic nor based on blood relations (as noted by the website Oxford Islamic Studies Online).

41   Samarkand is located in east-central Uzbekistan and is considered one of the oldest cities in Central Asia. According to the Encyclopedia Britannica (online), Samarkand has been ruled by a range of rulers including Alexander the Great (4th century), Central Asian Turks (6th century), Arabs (8th century), Samanids (9th and 10th centuries), various Turkic peoples (11th-13th centuries), and the Russian Empire (19th and 20th centuries).

42   Passages in this section were first outlined in my Huff Post article titled "The Other Al-Andalus – When Muslims and Christians Flourished Side by Side in Sicily."

43   According to the Britannica Encyclopedia (online), the Normans were originally pagan barbarian pirates from Denmark, Iceland, and Norway who began to make destructive plundering raids on European coastal settlements in the 8th century.

44   Scarfiotti, Gian Luigi and Lunde, Paul. 1978. "Muslim Sicily." *Aramco World*, November/December. Retrieved online from https://archive.aramcoworld.com/issue/197806/muslim.sicily.htm.

45   More commonly known as H.G. Wells.

46   Passages in this section were first outlined in my Huff Post article titled "Rumi and Emerson: A Bridge Between the West and the Muslim World."

47   Sefik Can's book *Fundamentals of Rumi's Thought: A Mevlevi Sufi Perspective* (2006) sheds light on Rumi's life within the Islamic mystical tradition.

48   This quotation is not mentioned in the Qur'an. The epigraph used by Emerson is itself a revision, or perhaps a loose paraphrasing of comments made by Muhammad as documented in *The Practical Philosophy of the Muhammadan People: Being a Translation of the Akhlak-i-Jalaly (1839)*, a Persian source translated into

English, as Roger Sedarat pointed out on page 97 of *Emerson in Iran: The American Appropriation of Persian Poetry* (2019, SUNY Press).

49 See Russell B. Goodman's blog post, "Emerson and Islam." https://blog.oup.com/2015/07/emerson-islam/

50 Pierre Crabitès was appointed as a U.S. representative on the Mixed Courts of Cairo by President William H. Taft.

51 According to Oxford Reference (online), the Battle of the Camel took place in 656 between followers of Caliph Ali ibn Abi Talib and Meccan aristocrats led by Muhammad's wife, Aisha, protesting Ali's failure to capture and punish the murderers of his predecessor, Uthman. The battle, named for the camel on which Aisha sat, is the first battle in Islamic history in which the caliph actually led troops on the battlefield. See: https://www.oxfordreference.com/view/10.1093/oi/authority.20110803095544252

52 Myriam Francois-Cerrah's article in *The Guardian* separates fact from fiction about Muhammad's relationship with Aisha, which is sometimes used to peddle anti-Muhammad narratives.

53 The Arabic term *hijab* translates roughly to "veil." It refers to something that conceals, covers, or protects against penetration between two things (Considine 2019: 74).

54 Passages in this section were first outlined in my Huff Post article titled "The Problem With Banning the Burqa."

55 The Arabic term *hijab*, which translates roughly to "veil," refers to something that conceals, covers, or protects against penetration between two things (Considine 2019: 74). As a Muslim woman's code of dress, *hijab* refers to a loose cloth or head-covering scarf worn by some women in public to cover her *'awrah*, an Arabic term denoting the parts of the body that should be covered for the sake of "modesty."

56 Passages in this section were first outlined in my Huff Post article titled "Jesus Christ and Prophet Muhammad Followed 'The Golden Rule.'"

57 These parts of Asian Minor included the provinces of Bithynia, Cappadocia, Galatia, and Pontus.

58 According to its website (yaqeeninstitute.org), the Yaqeen Institute is a non-profit research initiative that aims to address relevant topics head-on with the help of the foremost experts in this space. The institute aims to be the trusted source regarding these topics by creating engaging content in various formats, including journals, papers, articles, surveys, videos, conferences, and curriculum.

59 Michael Wolfe offered this quote in *Muhammad: Legacy of a Prophet*, a film by Kikim Media and Unity Productions Foundation. This documentary premiered nationally on PBS on December 18th, 2002.

60 Passages in this section were first outlined in my Huff Post article titled "A New Perspective of 'Jihad' in Christianity and Islam."

61 This Gandhi quote was cited in a statement that he published in Young India in 1924.

62 Passages in this section were first outlined in my Huff Post article titled "Christians and Muslims Should Embrace 'The Jihad of Jesus.'"

63 Jesus, or *Isa*, as he is known in Arabic, is recognized and embraced as one of the most significant prophets and messengers of God according to the Qur'an (Considine 2019: 85). The Islamic holy text defines Jesus by several phrases including the "Spirit of God," the "Word from God," and "the Messiah." A Muslim cannot be a Muslim if they do not revere him. With that said, there are important distinctions regarding Jesus' divinity in the Christian and Islamic traditions (ibid). Muslims do not consider him to be the "Son of God," but rather a human being. The Qur'an also denies the mainstream Christian belief that Jesus was crucified and resurrected (Considine 2019: 86).

64 Passages in this section were first outlined in my Huff Post article titled "An Unlikely Connection Between the Prophet Muhammad and George Washington."

65 These narrations were analyzed and re-recorded by Sidi Abdullah Anik Misra of the Global Islamic Seminary. Link: https://seekersguidance.org/answers/general-counsel/is-it-true-that-someone-threw-trash-on-the-prophet-peace-and-blessings-of-allah-be-upon-him/

66 This statement is attributed to the *hadith* collections of Muslim and Bukhari.

67 Originally published in 1978, Michael Hart's book *The 100* "does not rank the greatest people, but the most influential, the people who swayed the destinies of millions of human beings, determined the rise and fall of civilizations, changed the course of history."

68 K.S. Ramakrishna Rao offered this quote in a pamphlet titled *Mohammad: The Prophet of Islam* (Issue 86, Edition 2). The pamphlet was published by World Assembly of Muslim Youth.

69 This is Prophet Muhammad's own uncle who became Muslim shortly before the Final Sermon.

INDEX